HOMES ON HOLD

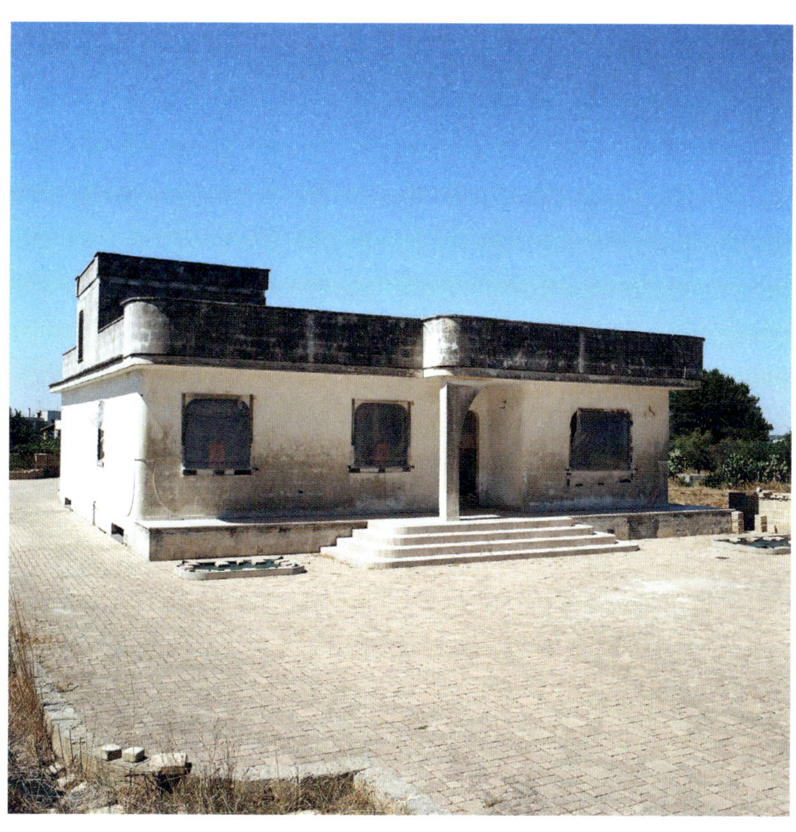

2013 - 2021

SALENTO

GABRIEL MAURON

This peninsula interspersed with villages is scattered with homes that have been put on hold. Some are under construction, while others have been abandoned amid the wild and arid countryside. They often stand alone. Their distinct decor is highlighted by the candid light and emerges from the barren land. They lend rhythm to the landscape, incorporating it and participating in its transformation.

Each new visit brings the hope of seeing an evolution, a change, a development. But construction does not always move forward in this region. The first building photographed for this project has been at a standstill for 10 years, without any progress. The son of the owner has moved up north. The site remains perpetually frozen and it no longer makes sense to invest in the project.

These houses reflect the fragility of a dream. A dream that sometimes remains suspended, forever lingering in the oppressive heat. In the middle of summer, they languish under the burdensome sun, taking part in the general torpor. But they are also evidence of personal sacrifice and a creativity that brims over and has no fixed rules. What may be perceived as an error thus becomes a source of inspiration.

The buildings have little to say and elicit only brief discussions. Their stories are shrouded in silence. The uncertainty that surrounds them incites our imagination to wander and to wonder: what would life have been like within them?

It was important for me to re-position these home-building projects in the human context that gave rise to them. Upon my request, inhabitants of the region came to the sites of these homes under construction. They are not the owners, but I immortalize their presence on these sites. They share their perspectives and their impressions, attesting to a great deal of patience and another manner of approaching time. This work renders homage to the "Salentini" and their unflagging desire to construct their own future.

Minervino di Lecce

Poggiardo

Sanarica

Cocumola

Giurdignano

Cerfignano

Moromonte

Alimini

Palmariggi

Soleto

Cannole

Vitigliano

Muro Leccese

Uggiano la Chiesa

Casamassella

Zollino

San Cassiano

Scorrano

Giuggianello

Barbarano del Capo

Otranto

Porto Badisco

Spongano

Porto Tricase

Sternatia

Specchia Gallone

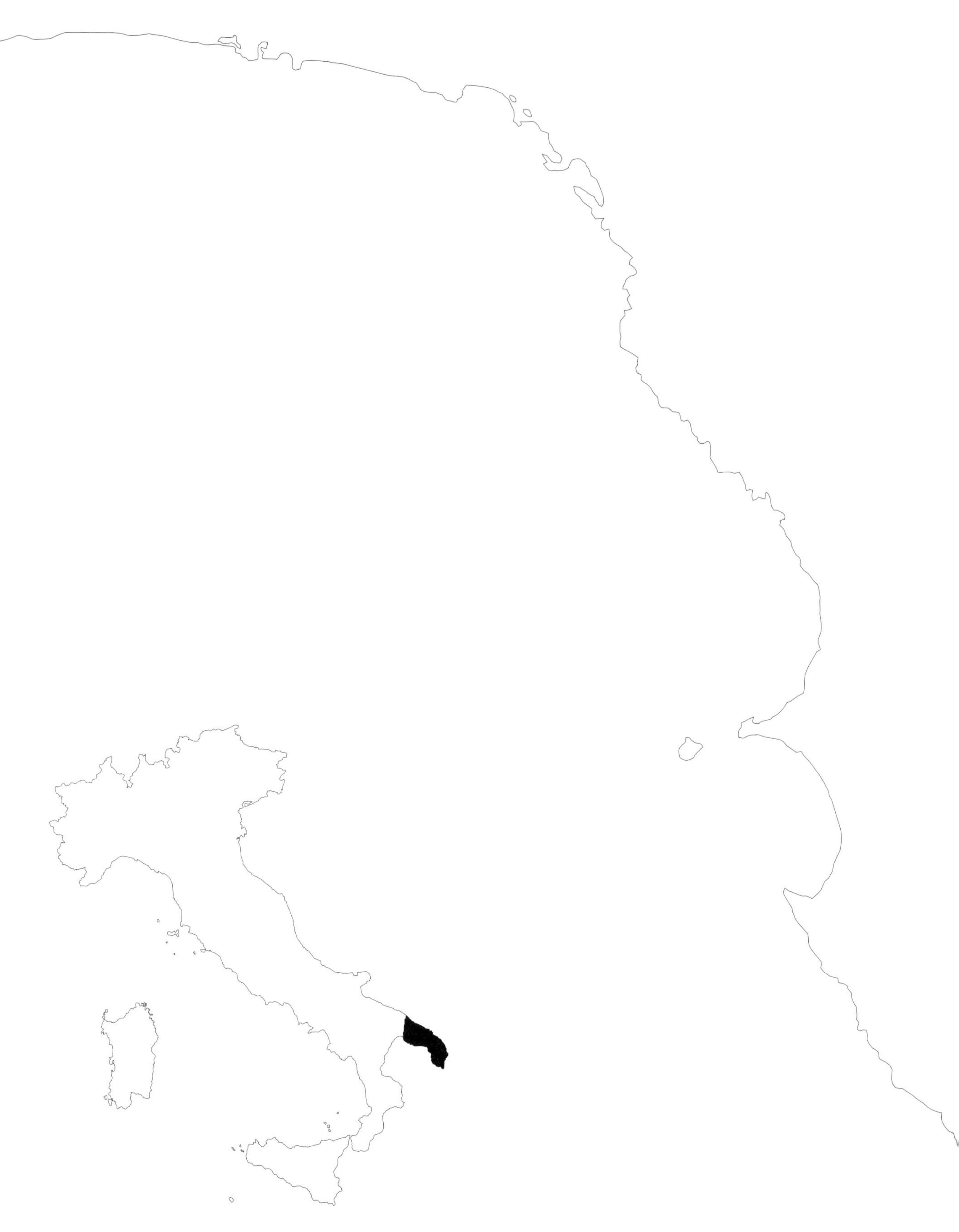

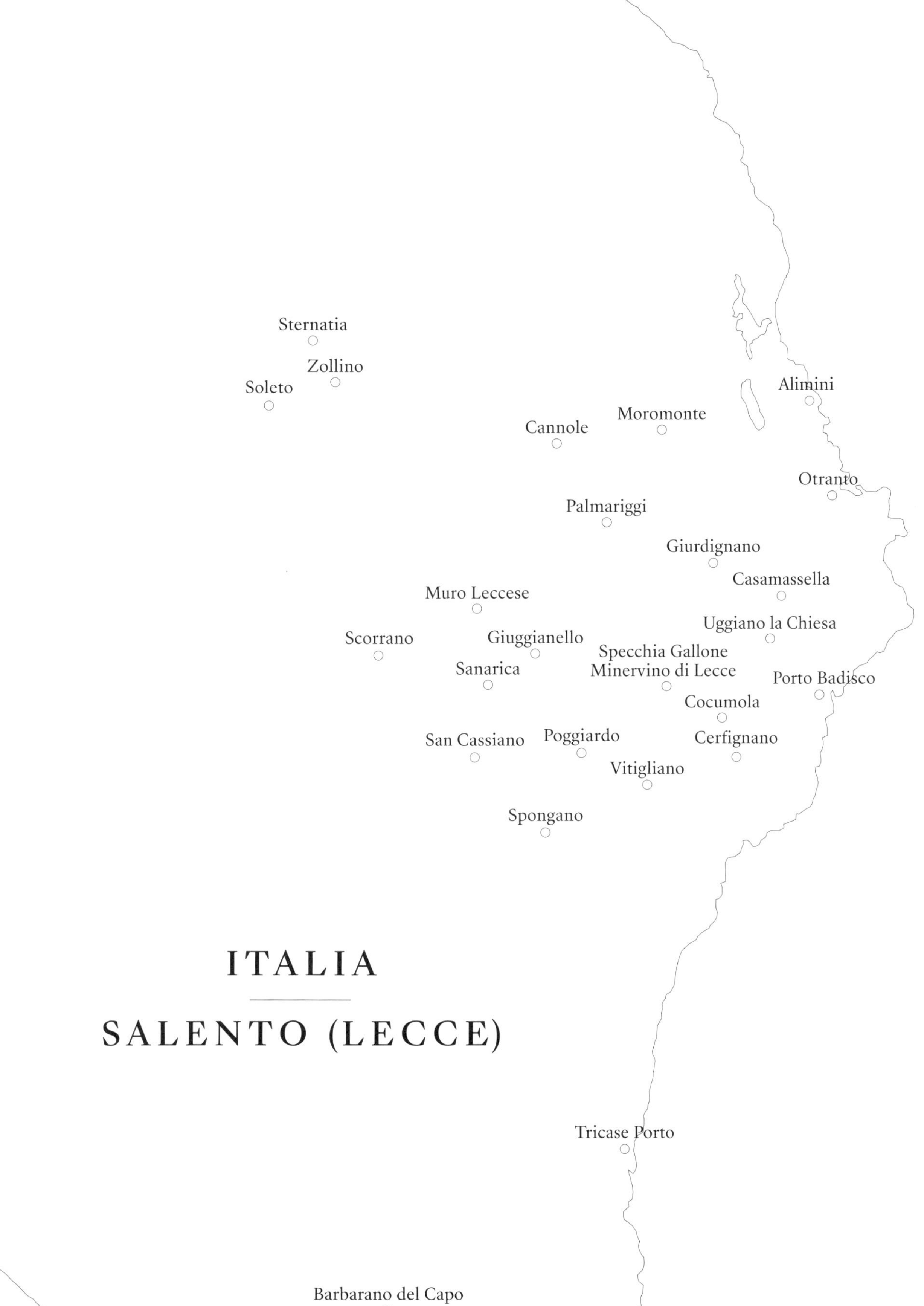

Sternatia
Zollino
Soleto
Alimini
Moromonte
Cannole
Otranto
Palmariggi
Giurdignano
Casamassella
Muro Leccese
Uggiano la Chiesa
Scorrano
Giuggianello
Specchia Gallone
Sanarica
Minervino di Lecce
Porto Badisco
Cocumola
San Cassiano
Poggiardo
Cerfignano
Vitigliano
Spongano
ITALIA
SALENTO (LECCE)
Tricase Porto
Barbarano del Capo

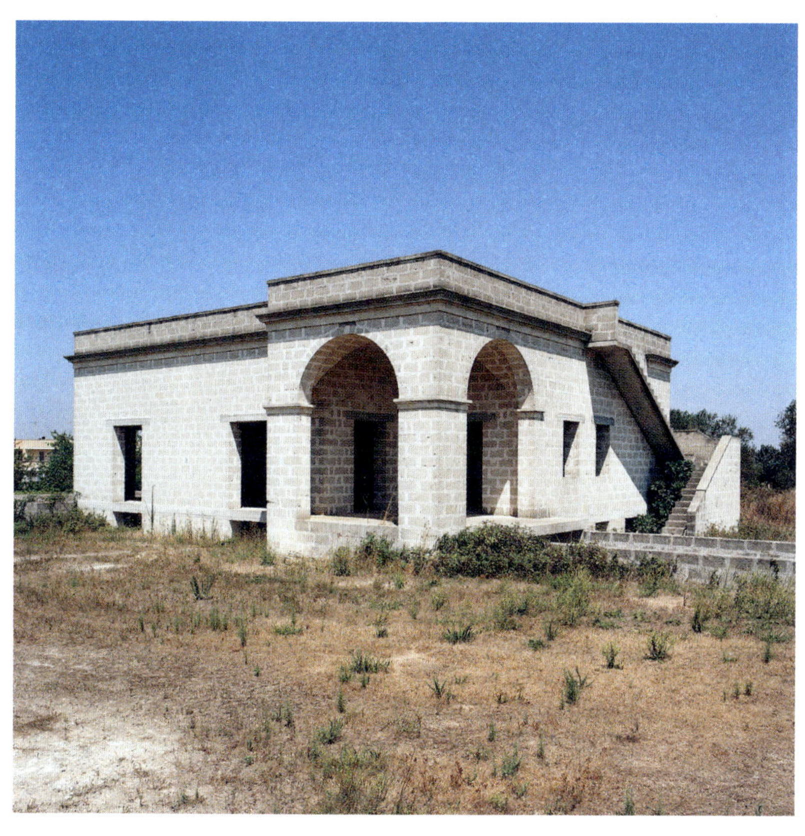

MINERVINO DI LECCE

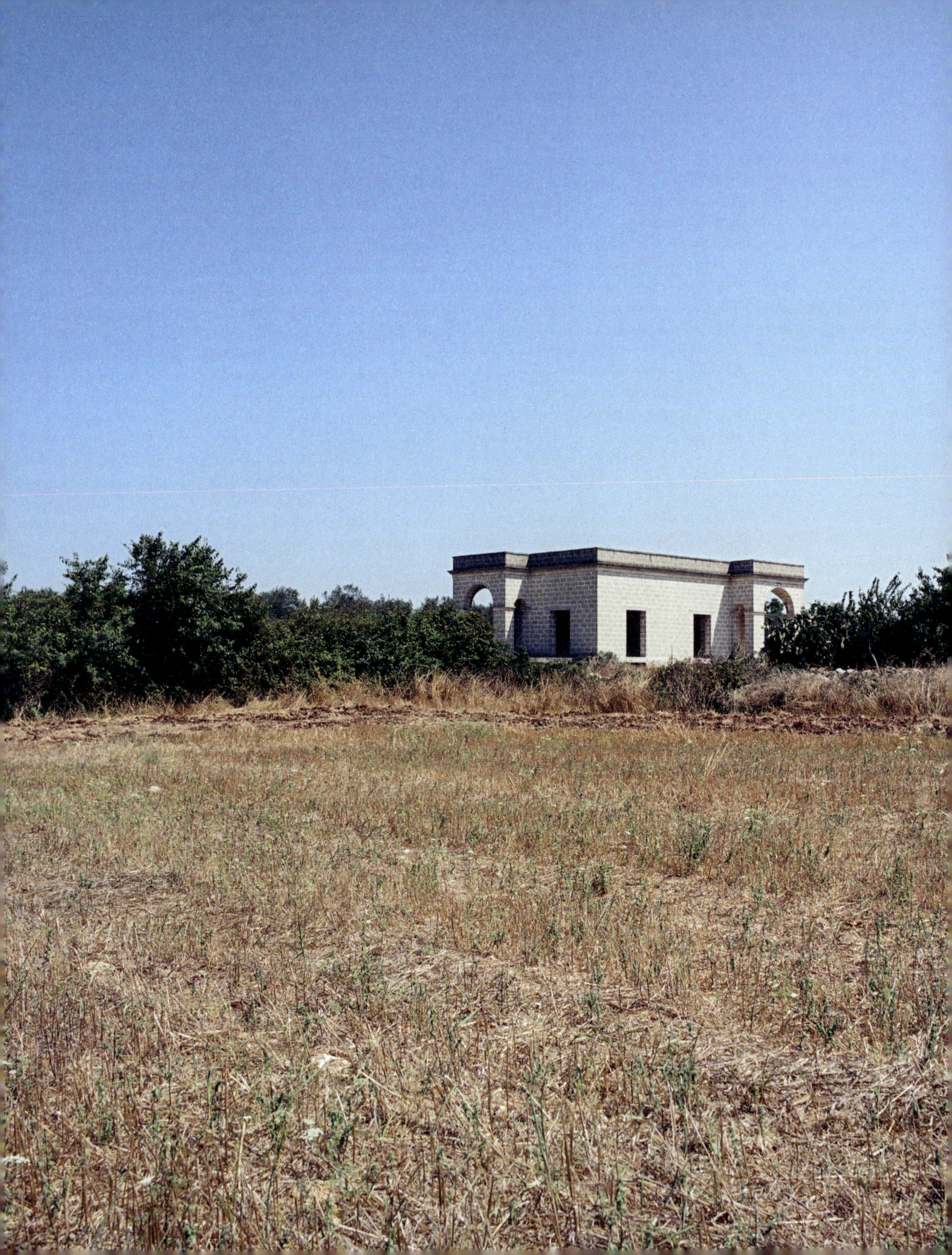

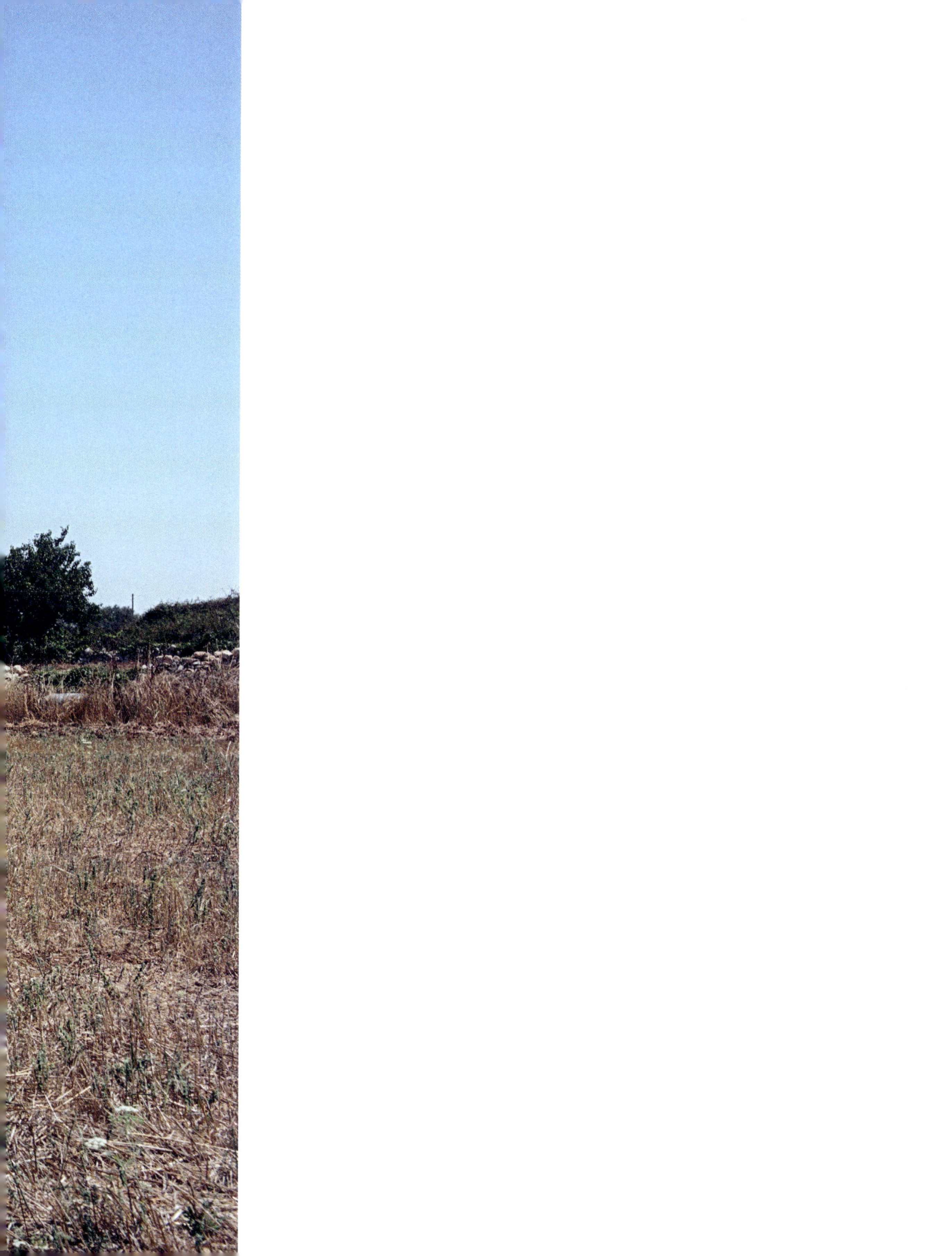

THE AESTHETICS OF DESIRE

Francesca Giofrè, Fabio Quici
Faculty of Architecture, Sapienza University of Rome

According to a survey recently conducted by CRESME (Centro di Ricerche Economiche, Sociologiche e di Mercato), a research centre that provides information for those working in the building and construction industry in Italy, there are around 15 billion buildings on Italian territory, 11.9 million of which are intended for residential or mixed use (residential and commercial). The survey also reveals the predominance of residential constructions that are "low and diminutive, composed of buildings of small and very small dimensions", with around 9.1 million of them in total.

In order to have a better understanding of the quality of these constructions, it is important to note that 41% of these homes are self-designed, or designed in situ by the construction companies; 40% are the work of surveyors, who, under Italian legislation, have the right to design modest homes without a diploma of higher education or, even more significantly, adequate knowledge of architecture; 11% are designed by architects; and 8% by engineers. While Italy may be the country with the highest number of practicing architects (2.5 for every thousand residents), these percentages contrast with a reality in which buildings are being erected by professionals in construction who do not have any true knowledge of architecture.

Added to this is the persistent phenomenon of illegal construction. According to the most recent data provided by ISTAT (Italian National Institute of Statistics), there are about 20 unauthorized constructions for every 100 authorized ones in Italy, with the phenomenon concentrated above all in the central and southern regions of the country. The reasons for unauthorized construction are varied and concern both politics and social customs. A recent draft law that, fortunately, was abandoned called for recognizing a distinction between illegal construction borne out of so-called "necessity" and illegal construction for speculation, in order to spare illegal homes from being demolished, which some seek to justify on the basis of a lack of financial resources and the need for housing. In reality, the majority of illegal houses in Italy are second homes or vacation homes that remain empty during the year and are located in coastal zones or have some other touristic value.

Another widespread phenomenon in Italy is the presence of unfinished buildings on the territory, whether they are state or private entities. In 2015, there was estimated to be 838 publicly owned buildings that remain unfinished (see Anagrafe delle Opere pubbliche Incompiute), 45% of which are clustered in four regions: 113 in Sicily, 90 in Campania, 91 in Puglia and 80 in Sardegna. A 2016 legislative decree identifies these constructions as a priority and states that they must either be completed or some other solution must be found, for example by repurposing, downsizing, selling or demolishing them. Conversely, there is no legislation that obliges private parties to do the same.

Why do some buildings remain unfinished? There are many reasons, including a lack of funding, technical reasons, new technical norms or legal provisions, bankruptcy, contract termination and a lack of motivation to finish them.

Gabriel Mauron's photographs of these constructions in Salento are an illustration of the situation described above, but they also bring to light a paradox. Despite widespread urbanization in Italy, like the kind that can be observed in Salento, "architectural culture" has chosen to ignore the presence of these unfinished buildings and has never truly investigated the nature of and social, economic, aesthetic and functional reasons behind these constructions, which are considered to be devoid of any authorship that would make them worthy of note.

Once again, photography is drawing our attention to what lies at the margins.

When all eyes were turned to the modern boulevards traced out by Haussman, Eugène Atget documented the old alleys of Paris. Berenice Abbott turned her lens to an everyday existence that was on the point of vanishing in a rapidly changing Manhattan. Walker Evans documented wood constructions in rural America and small roadside businesses, preserving the memory of an American tradition. Bernd and Hilla Becher brought dignity to "anonymous sculptures" in industrial settings, documenting the anonymous and chaotic towns that arise in the outskirts of the big metropolises of the world, paying particular attention to the social dimension of an urban phenomenon that is bursting with life.

In Salento, the abandoned and suspended construction sites of the houses captured by Gabriel Mauron tell another story. Behind the numbers and the statistics, behind the variety of forms of these unfinished homes, we can conjure up stories of emigration and the projection of desires, a will to belong to the territory itself and an affirmation of a social condition.

In the sixties, around 17,000 people emigrated from Puglia to the north of Italy, flocking to Turin in particular. From 2008 to present day, approximately 20,000 people under the age of 30 have emigrated from Puglia. Many of these emigrants have maintained a deep relationship with their land of origin and this relationship has expressed itself in the form of a house that has been constructed and designed to fit with one particular desire – the desire to return home. Many of these houses belong to a population that no longer resides there. Their construction advances slowly in time, as economic circumstances change, along with desires. Lacking a definitive design, some of their forms reflect a progress that has been diluted by time. As elements have been gradually added, some of the houses appear to be the whimsical sum of inspirations taken from here and there, then assembled to form a whole that is far from uniform. Lacking any traits that are truly typical of the territory, these construction sites and homes draw on a repertoire of formal solutions derived from stereotypes and catalogues of ready-made components. And yet, even in the jumble of shapes and solutions documented in Gabriel's photographs, it is possible to discern an aesthetic: the aesthetic of desire. A desire to not only "live" but "exhibit" – exhibit the achievement of a better social condition, even far from populated areas, making use of agricultural land and demolishing traditional farm buildings to attain new dimensions. Often, they are second homes that are suspended in time and space, and do not enter into dialogue with the surrounding architecture, unless it is with one another.

Recurrent forms are produced out of cement, brick and sometimes local stone: flat roofs, terraces, loggias and patios. Cornices and stringcourse have at times been added to refine the stereometric proportions that are necessary to optimize the economy of construction. The homes often appear to be elevated on a platform above street level to accommodate garages and basements, complying with a culture of living in which "there is never enough space". Lowered rounded arches often frame the windows and punctuate the loggias, providing precious shade at a latitude at which one must protect oneself from the pitiless summer sun. Here and there, we can observe a lack of symmetry, as the building has been subject to continual reconsideration and adaptation in the course of construction in order to accompany the growth of families. In some cases, the cylinders that contain staircases rise from the exterior like medieval defense towers of a property that has ultimately been conquered after much labour and toil. Staircases, industrial balustrades and small columns of cement, as opposed to Lecce stone, seek to lend a certain nobility to these homes that may be expansive in dimension, swelling to match the aspirations of their owners, but modest in detail.

We can imagine the white-varnished plaster that will coat the building once it has been completed, softening its forms and dimensions, vouching for its livability and entering into a more traditional dialogue with the Mediterranean sun.

We need to suspend our judgment in order to probe the entropy of this suburban reality – "a land of the unfinished", with buildings suspended in nude structural dimensions and relegated to the territory of memory, thus contributing to "suburban accretion", an uncontrollable growth of artifacts attesting to individuals and the initiatives they undertake out of necessity or speculation. It is only then that we can make sense of the dissonant orchestration that often overrides all harmony. With our senses activated and the free associations that arise from these anthropogenic entities, amidst the cacophony and the silences, we can at times distinguish a line of construction that is nevertheless rooted in something that is, in its essence, familiar.

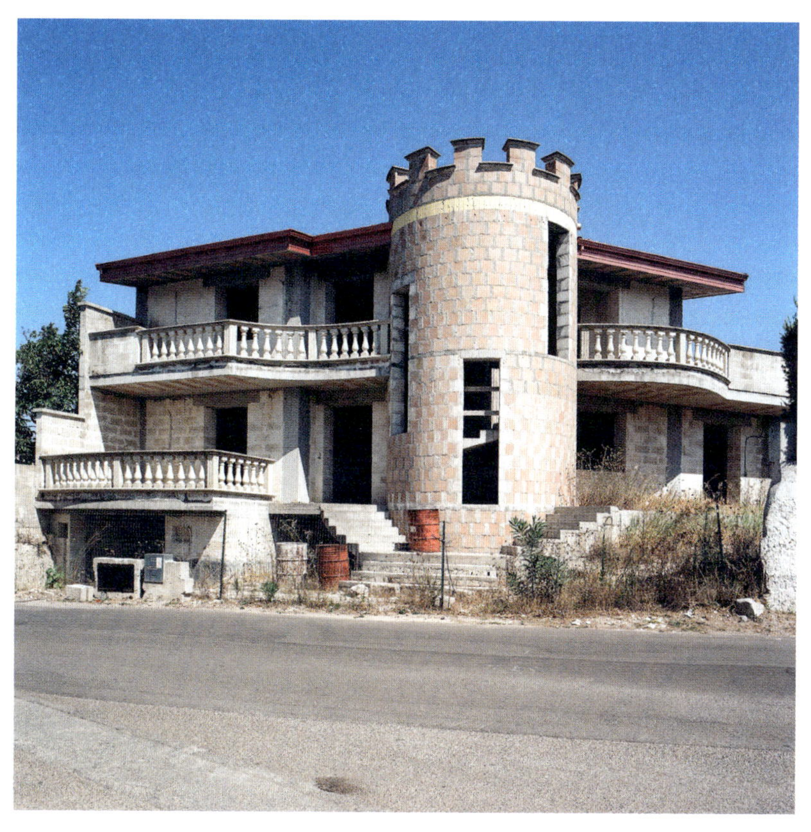

GIURDIGNANO

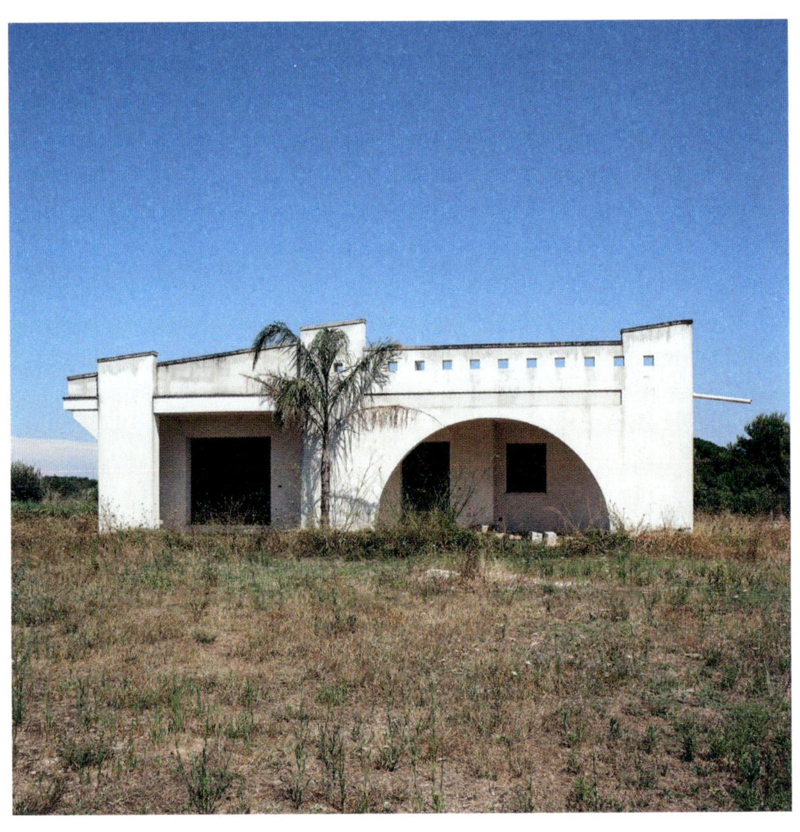

UGGIANO LA CHIESA

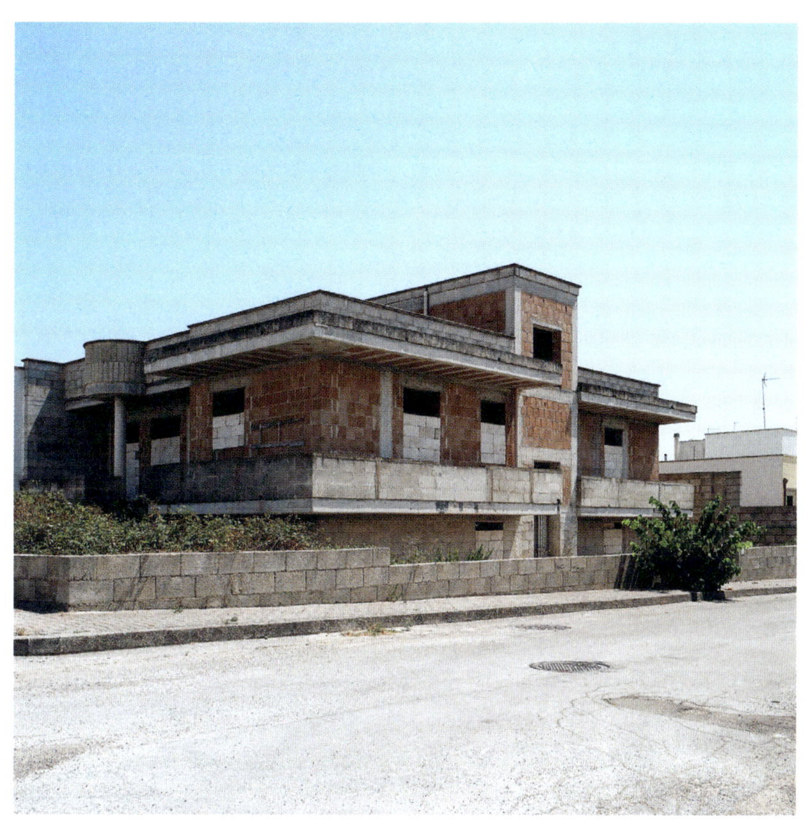

POGGIARDO

ANDREA

In Salento culture, there is a saying: "If you lay down one stone after another, you can erect a large wall". Even if it takes a long time, by making small and big sacrifices, a great dream can be achieved!

———

Nella nostra cultura salentina esiste un detto «pietra su pietra si erige un grande muro» anche se occorre molto tempo, con piccoli e grandi sacrifici si realizza un gran sogno!

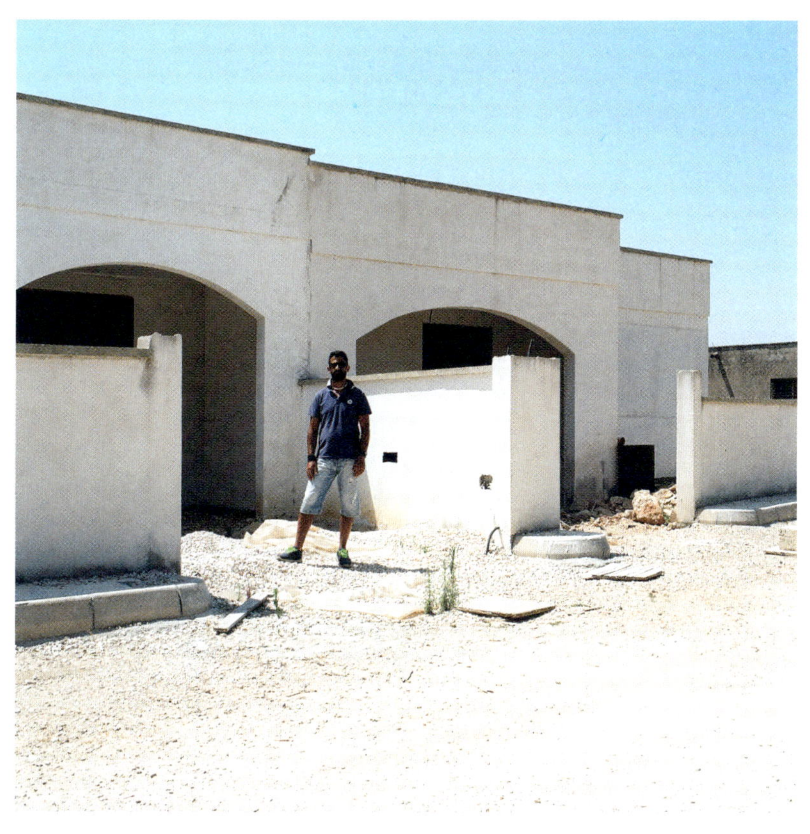

SPECCHIA GALLONE

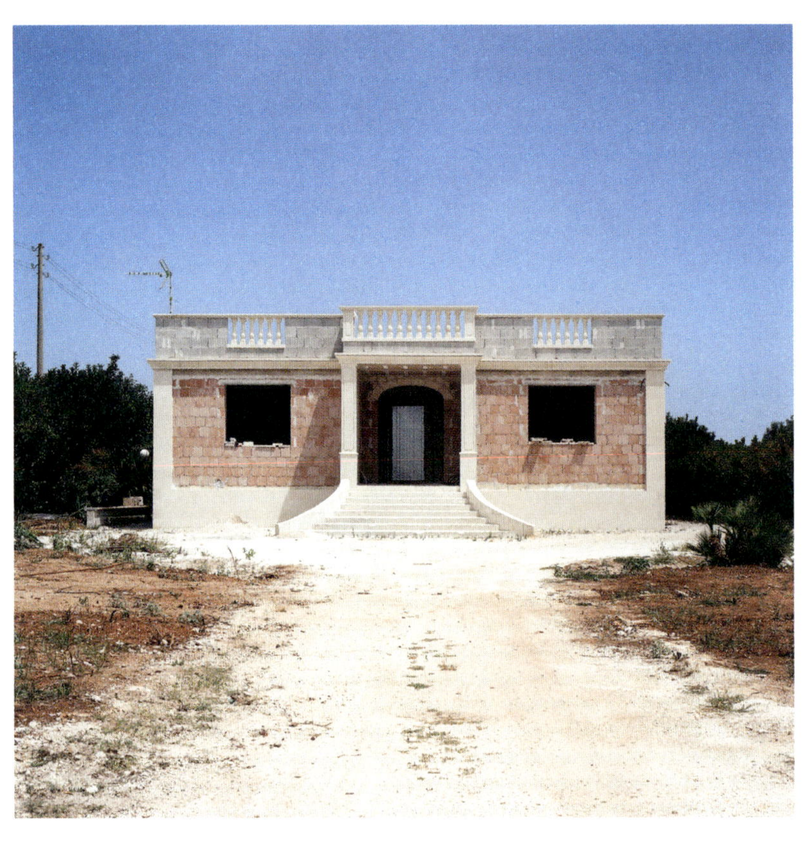

POGGIARDO

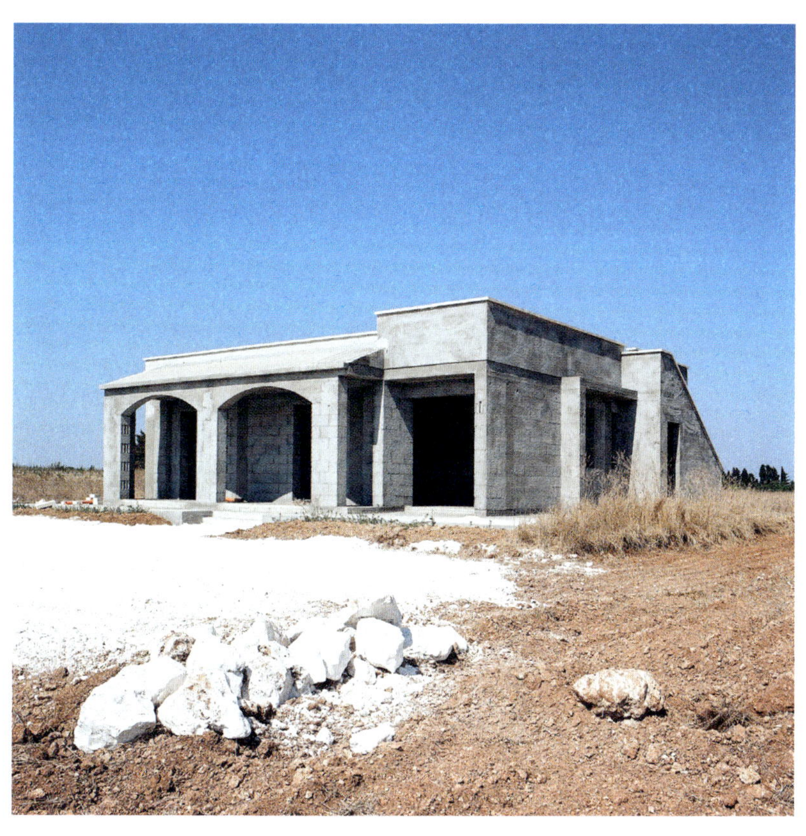

ALIMINI

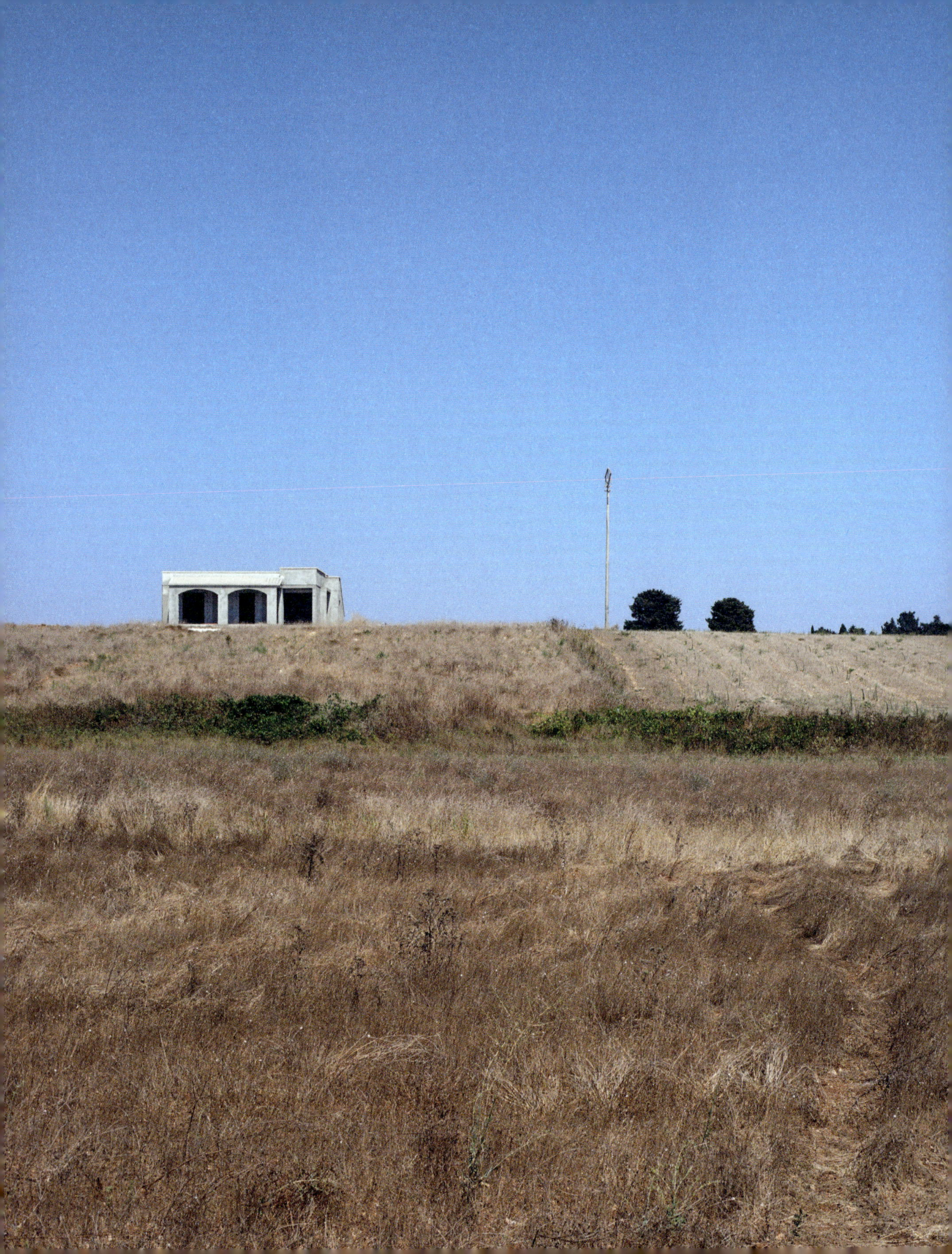

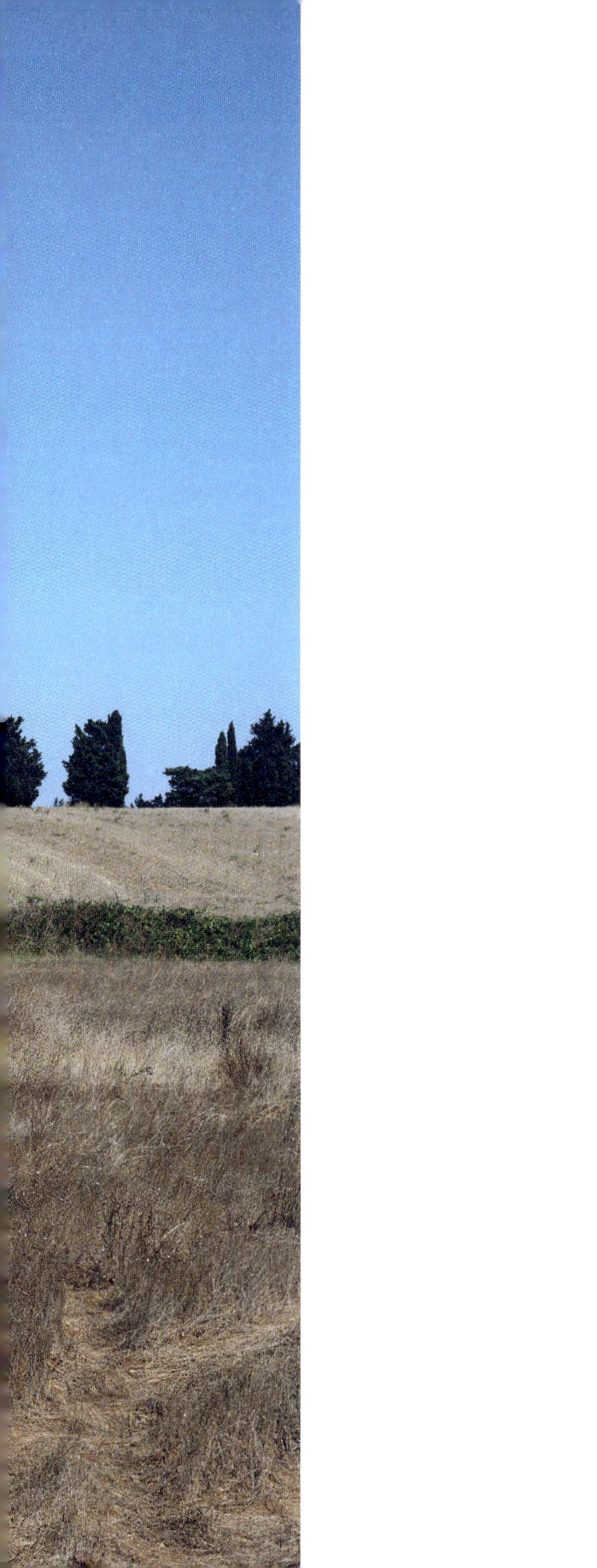

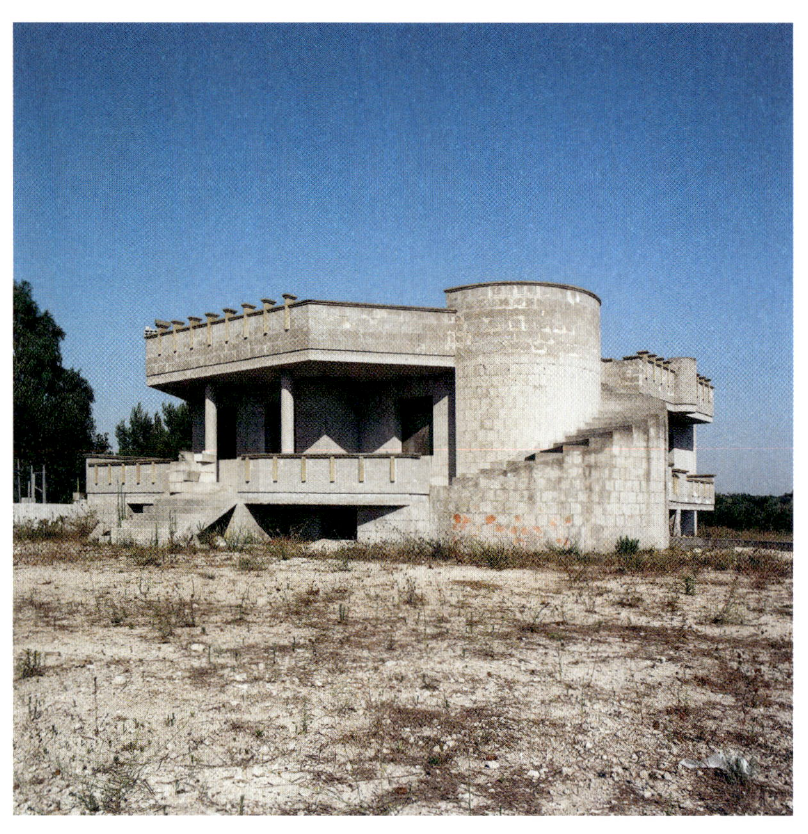

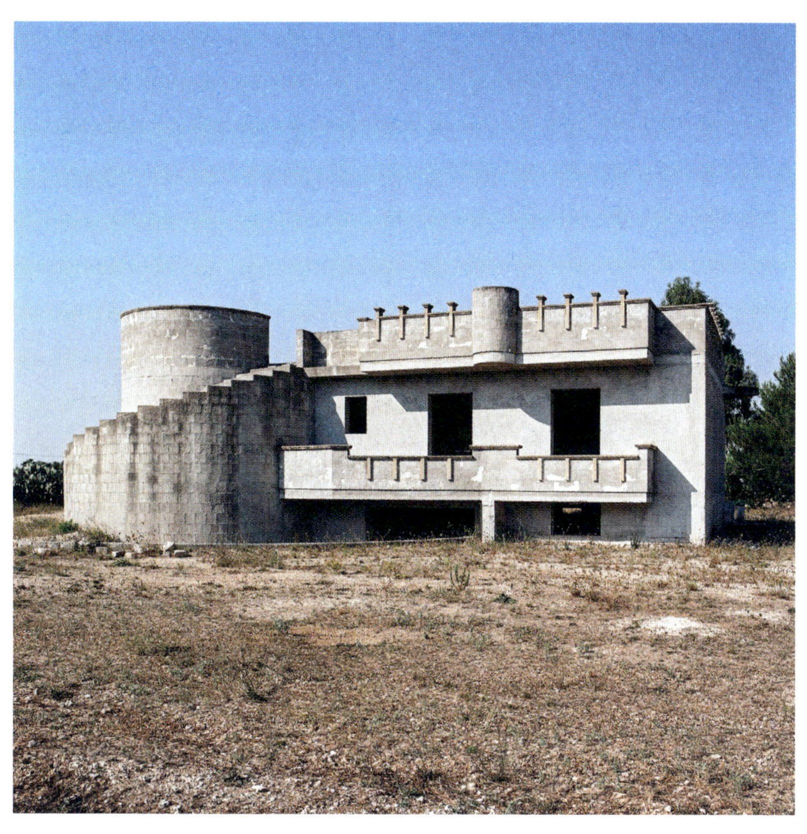

MURO LECCESE

PASQUALE

I don't consider these houses to be abandoned. Since it is my profession, I know that it takes a lot of time, money and patience to finish constructing them. Since the houses here are very big, the costs are very high.

———

Io non le considero delle case abbandonate perché essendo del mestiere so che ci vuole tempo, denaro e pazienza per ultimare i lavori. Qua le case sono molto grandi e di conseguenza i costi sono molto alti.

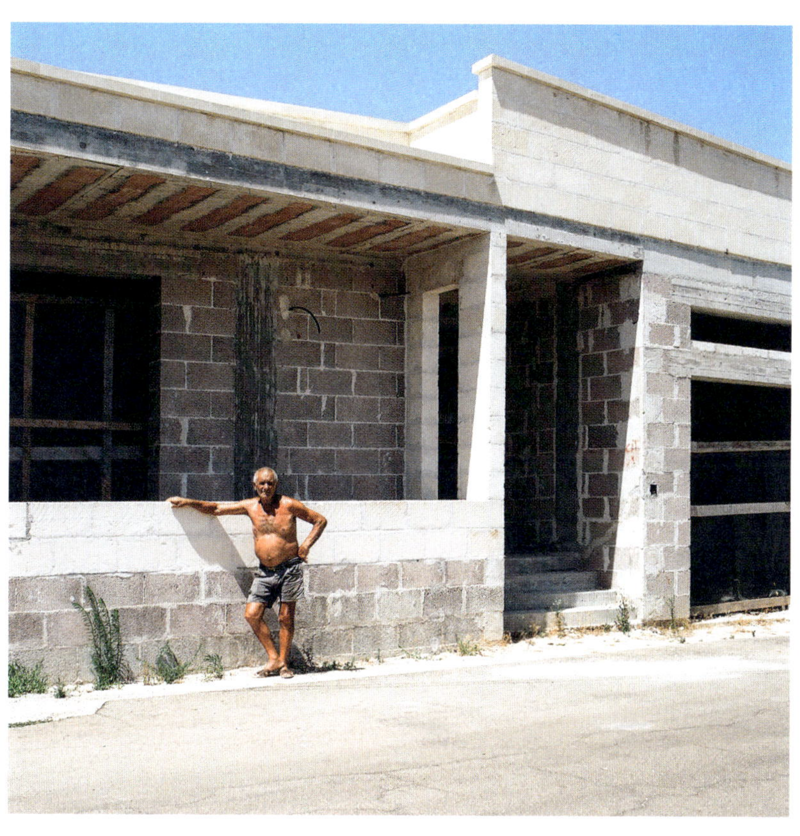

MINERVINO DI LECCE

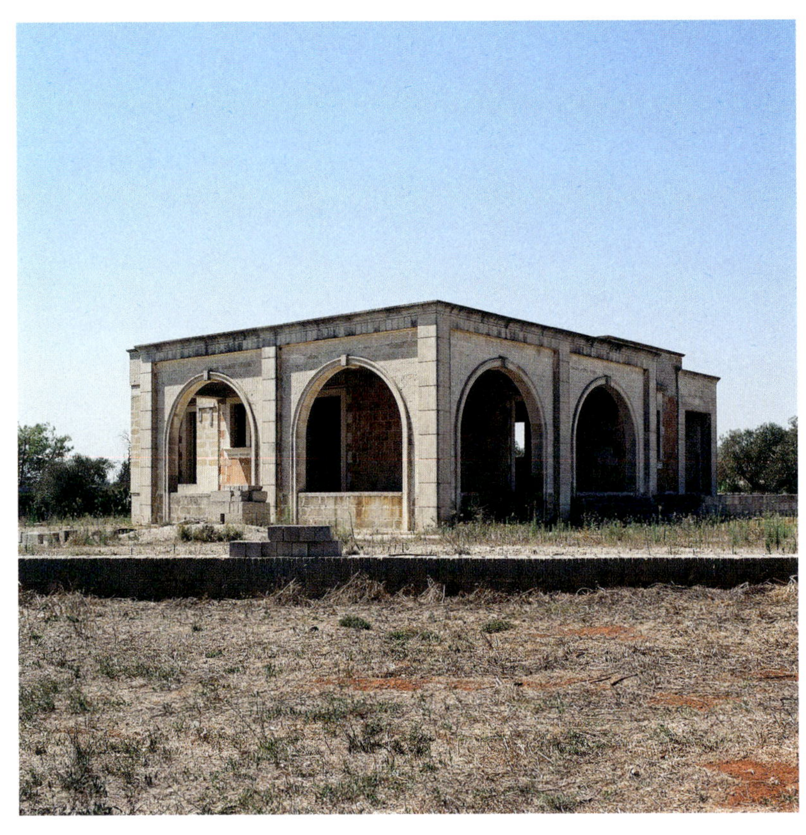

SANARICA

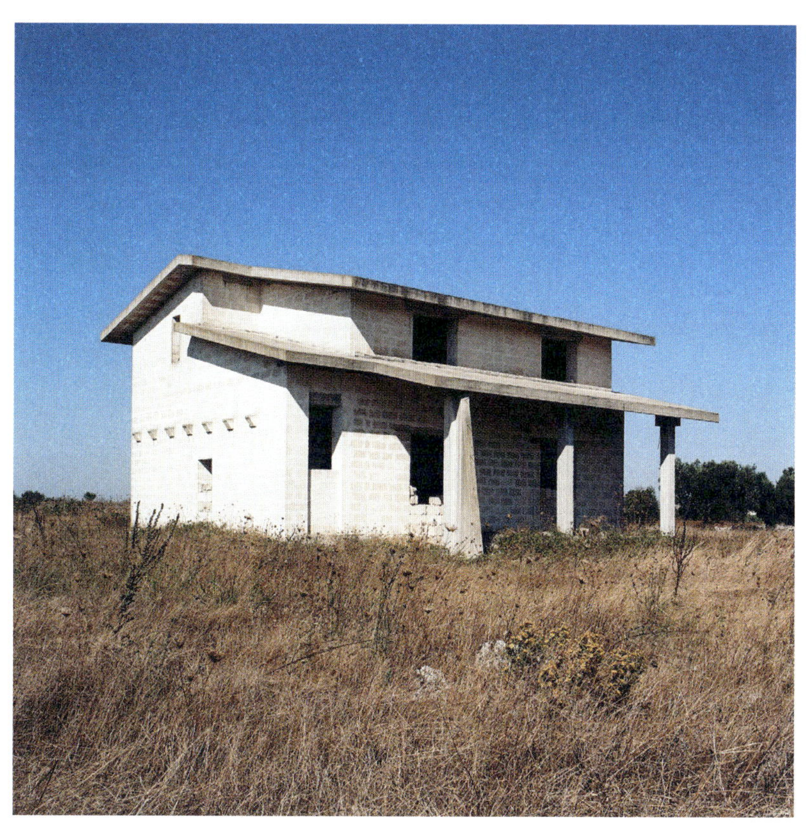

PALMARIGGI

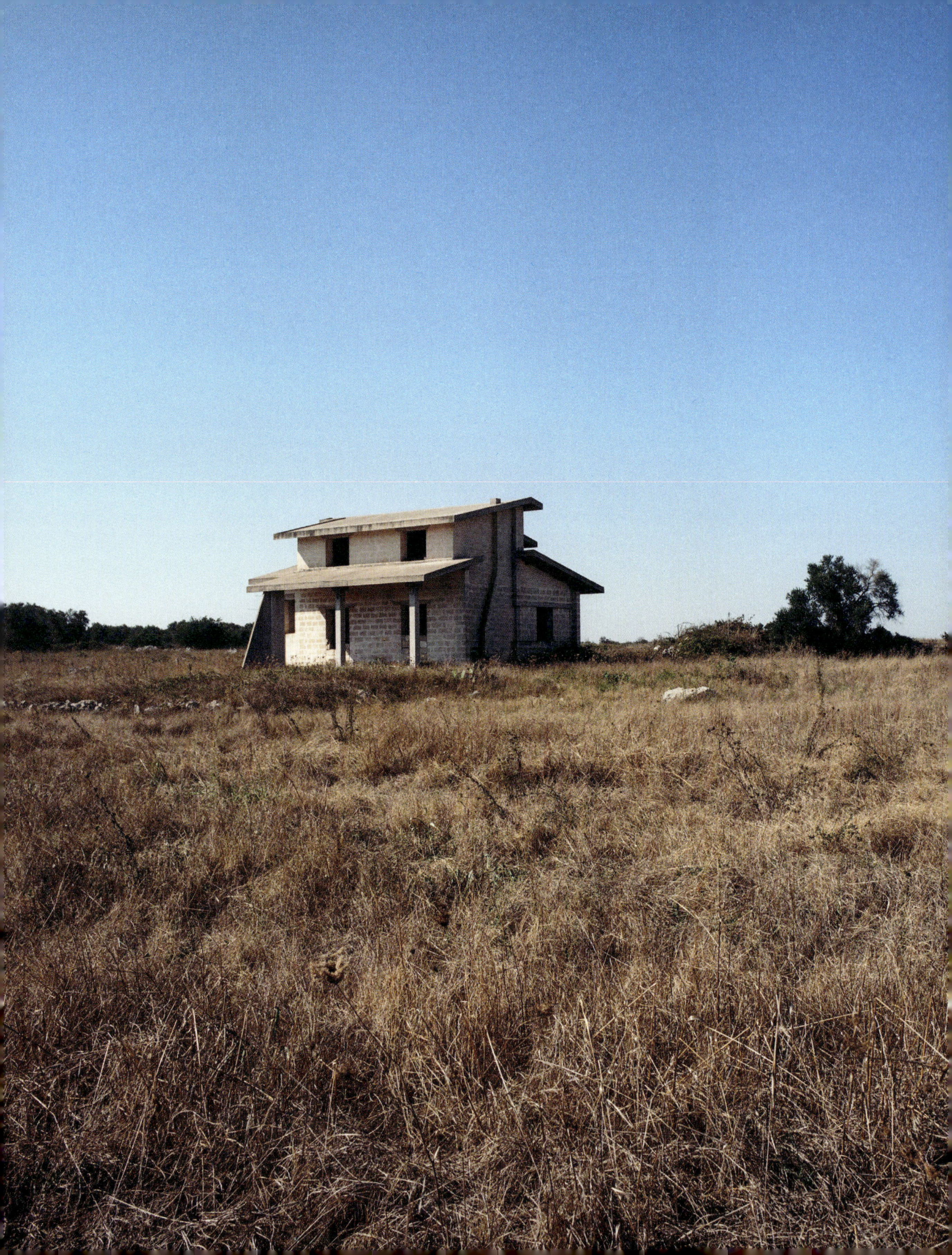

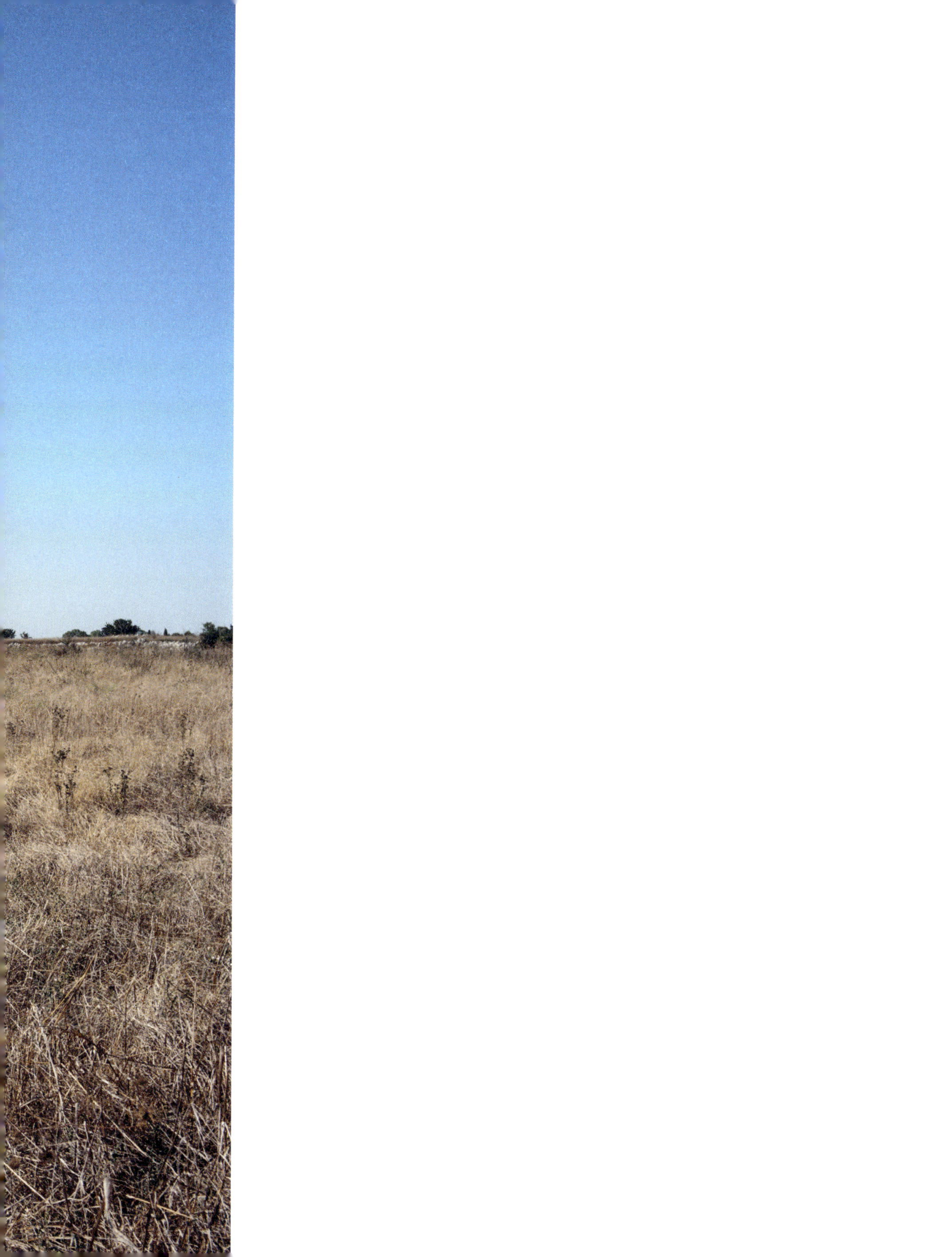

DONATELLA

For us, these rough houses are a waste because they are constructed so big out of delusions of grandeur, then the owners run out of money and are unable to complete them. They remain like that for years and years, getting worn down. What a waste! Such a sad sight!

Noi, di queste case in rustico, pensiamo che siano uno spreco perché le fanno grandi per manie di grandezza ma poi finiscono i soldi e non riescono a terminarle. Rimangono anni e anni così, a logorarsi. È uno spreco! Che tristezza!

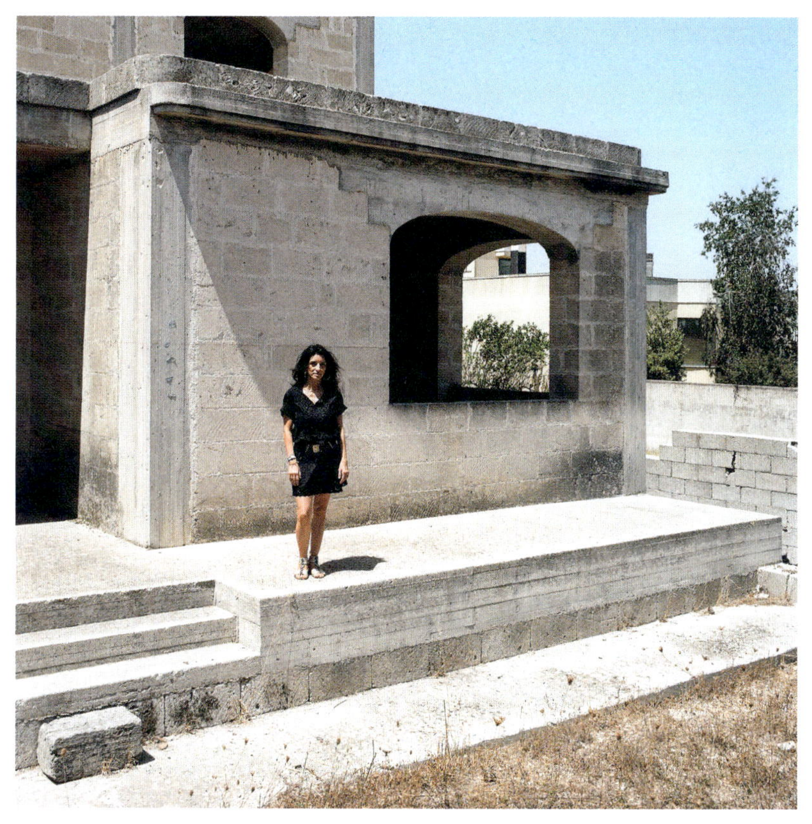

COCUMOLA

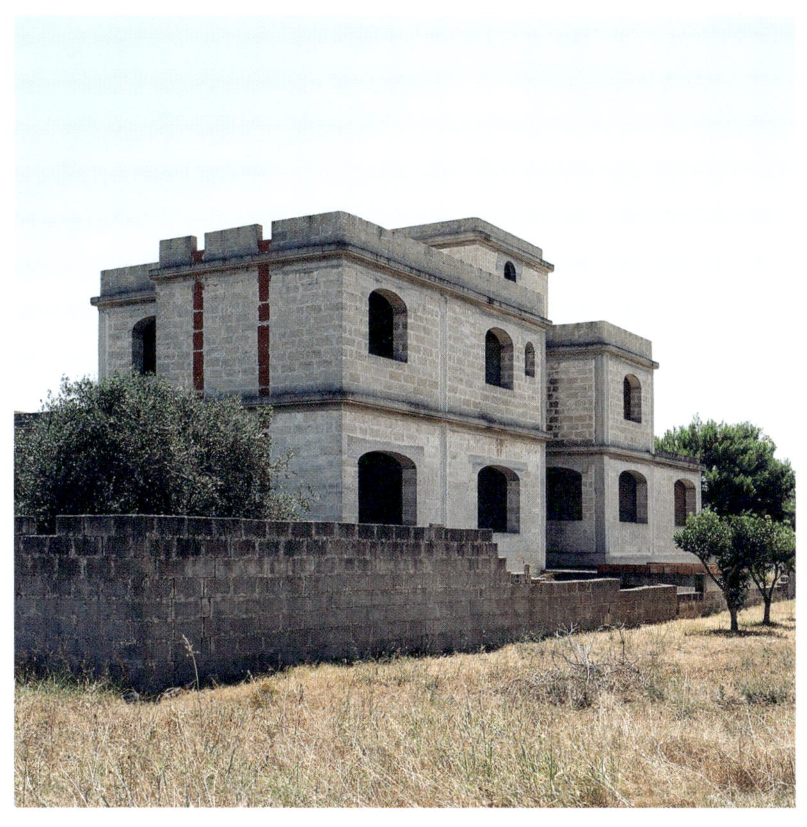

COCUMOLA

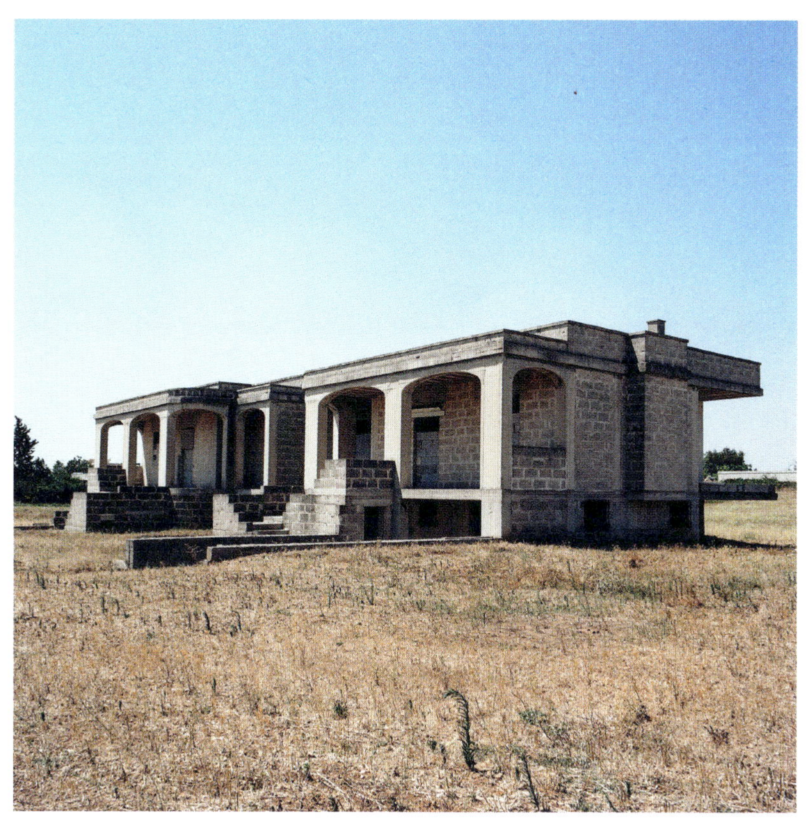

POGGIARDO

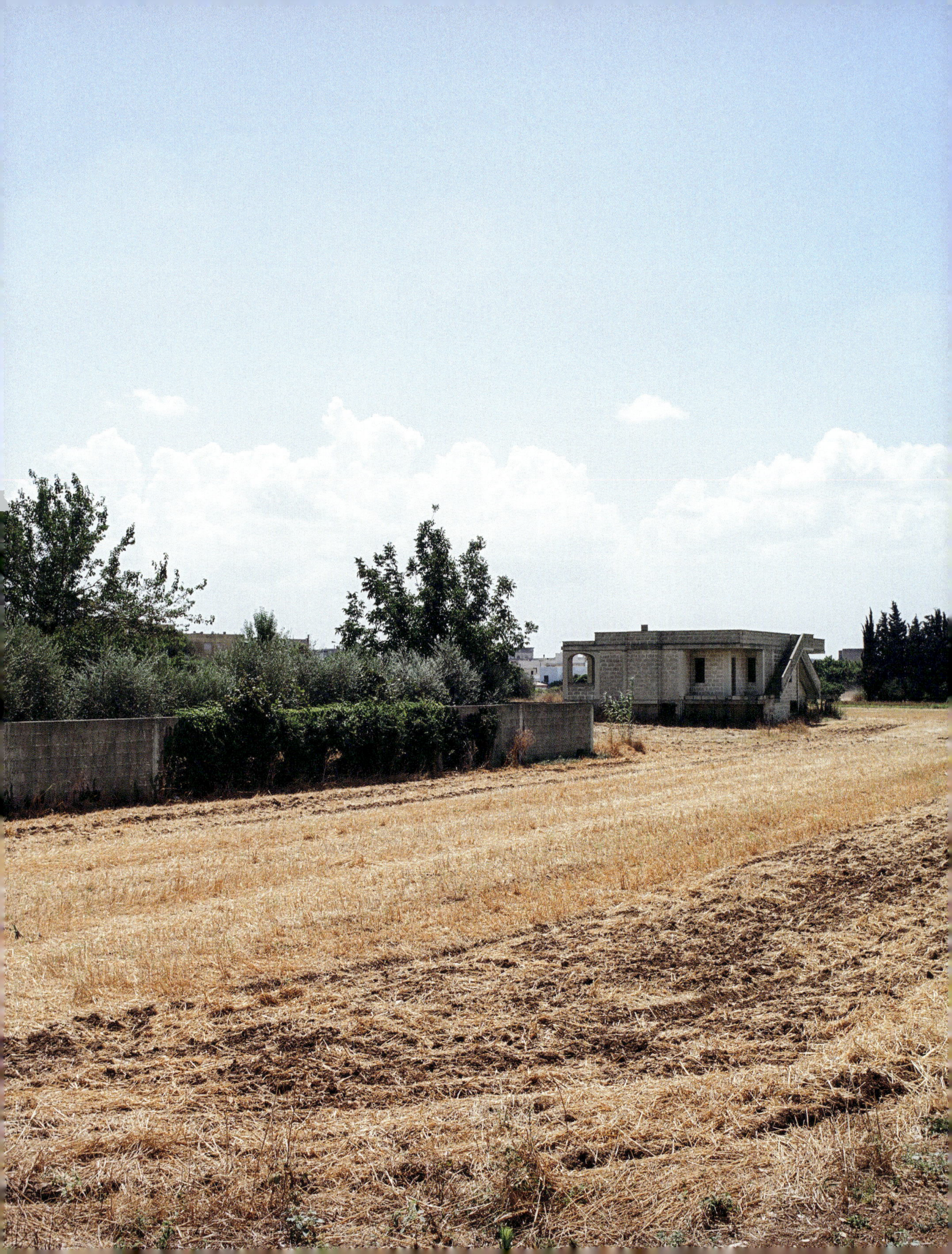

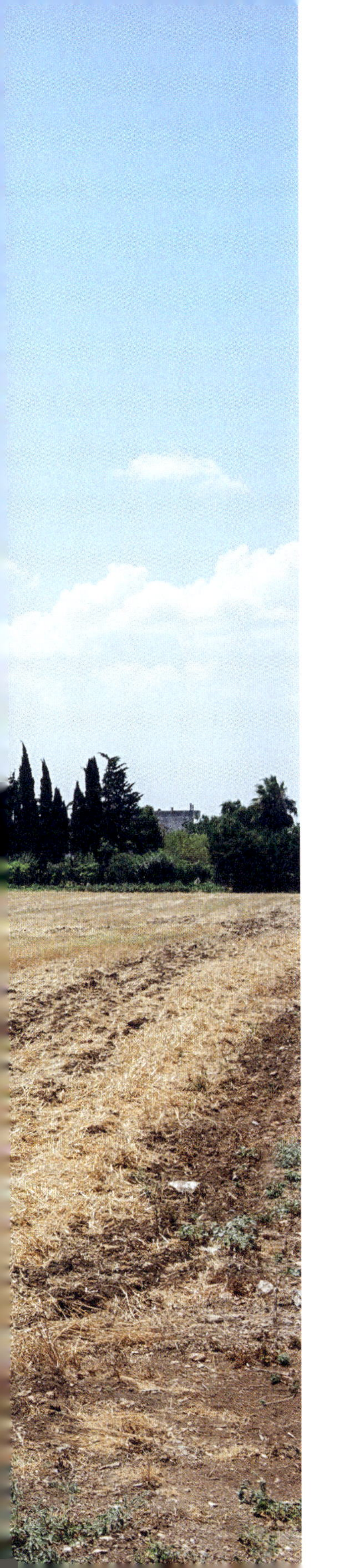

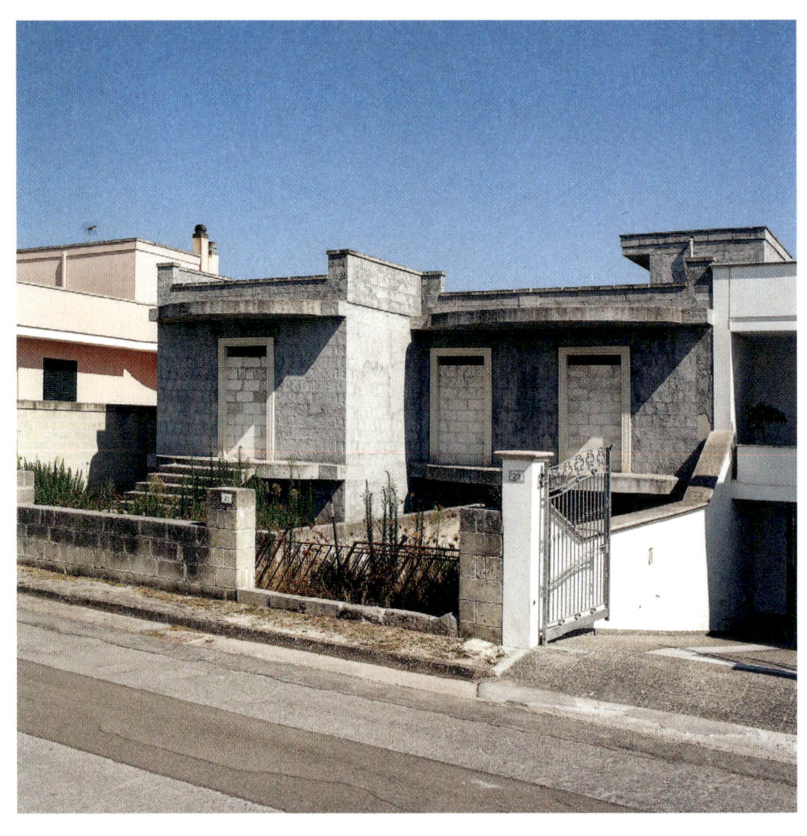

POGGIARDO

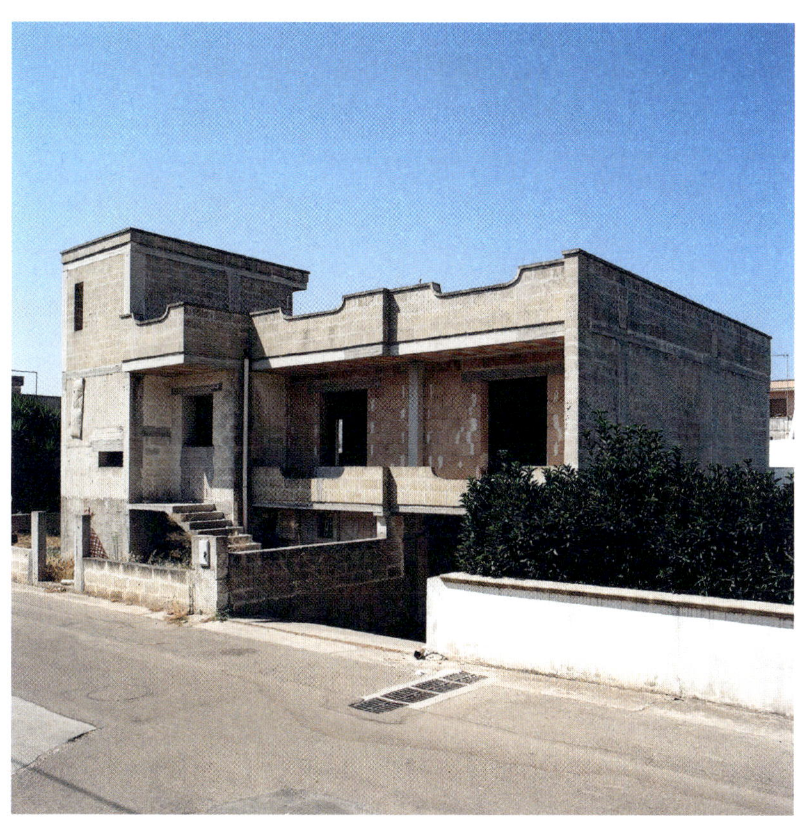

GIURDIGNANO

DONATO

Personally, I don't mind if they haven't been there for more than five years. In general, when you build a house, it's better, and even advisable, to wait three or four years. This time is necessary to lay down the foundations for the houses and install them on the land. Most future residents don't allow for this time for various reasons, then fissures begin to appear on the walls and the house is already weakened – so it's better to wait for three or four years.

When only the foundations have been laid down and there is no progress, these houses look like skeletons, and it cannot be denied that they ruin the landscape. And after a certain number of years – more than ten – these "beginnings" of houses are doomed and can no longer be salvaged. They are damaged by the weather and humidity, and it becomes impossible to maintain them. There is only one thing left to do: destroy them. Each time one is destroyed, the hopes of a family vanish. Many of my friends from the region have constructed their houses little by little, investing the money that they have saved up. Even if it takes more time, many of them have done the work themselves to save on costs.

———

A me, per esempio, non importa se non sono più di 5 anni. Perché in generale, quando si costruisce una casa, è preferibile e persino consigliabile aspettare 3-4 anni. Questo tempo è vantaggioso per le fondamenta della casa che si insediano sul terreno durante i primi anni. La maggior parte dei futuri abitanti non rispetta questo limite di tempo per vari motivi, le crepe compaiono non appena appaiono sui muri, e la casa si indebolisce (quindi è bene aspettare 3-4 anni).

Quando si gettano solo le fondamenta delle case e non c'è continuità, sembra uno scheletro di casa ed è innegabile che rende il paesaggio brutto. Inoltre, quello che è triste, è che dopo un certo numero di anni (più di 10 anni), questi «inizi di case» sono condannati, non possiamo più recuperarli. Sono danneggiati dal maltempo (umidità) e la manutenzione diventa impossibile, resta solo una cosa da fare: distruggerle. E in ogni distruzione purtroppo la speranza di una famiglia svanisce. Da parte mia, molti amici del paese hanno costruito le loro case poco a poco, investendo i soldi che hanno risparmiato. Anche se ci vuole più tempo, in tanti hanno fatto il lavoro da soli per risparmiare.

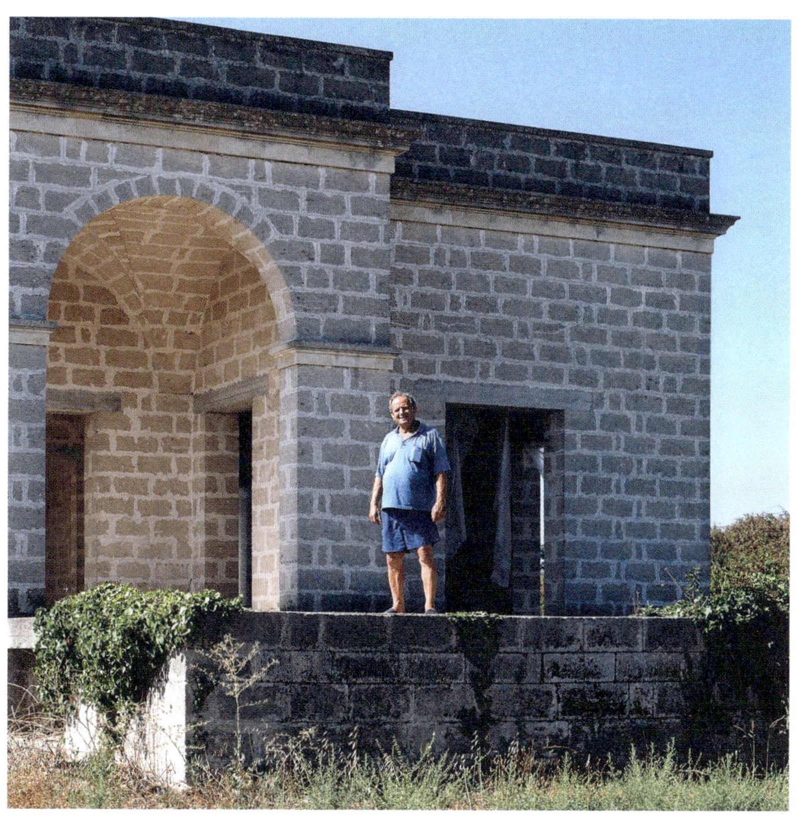

MINERVINO DI LECCE

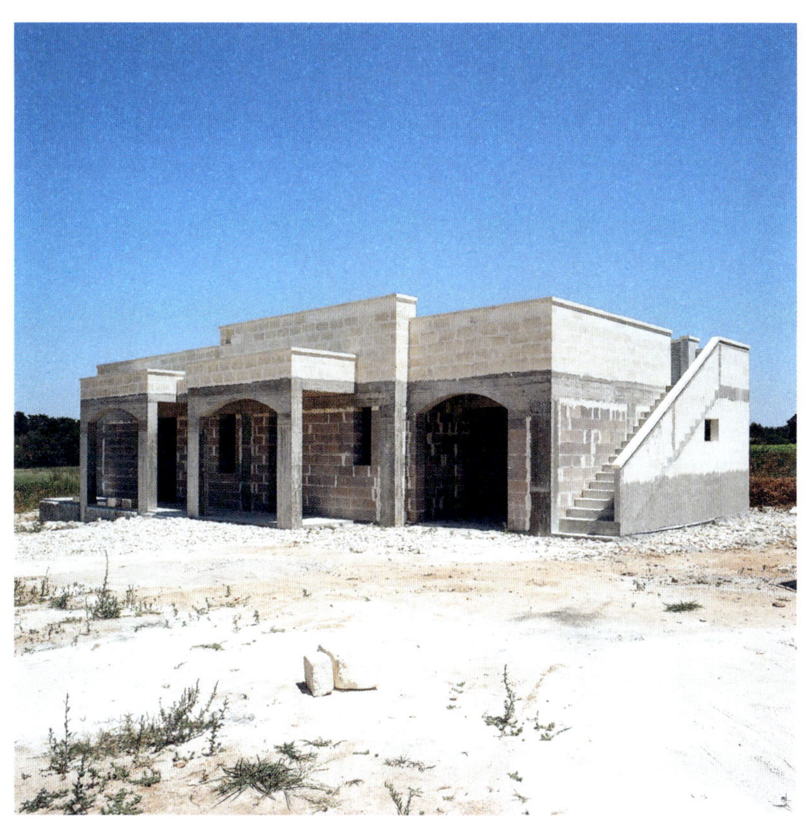

MOROMONTE

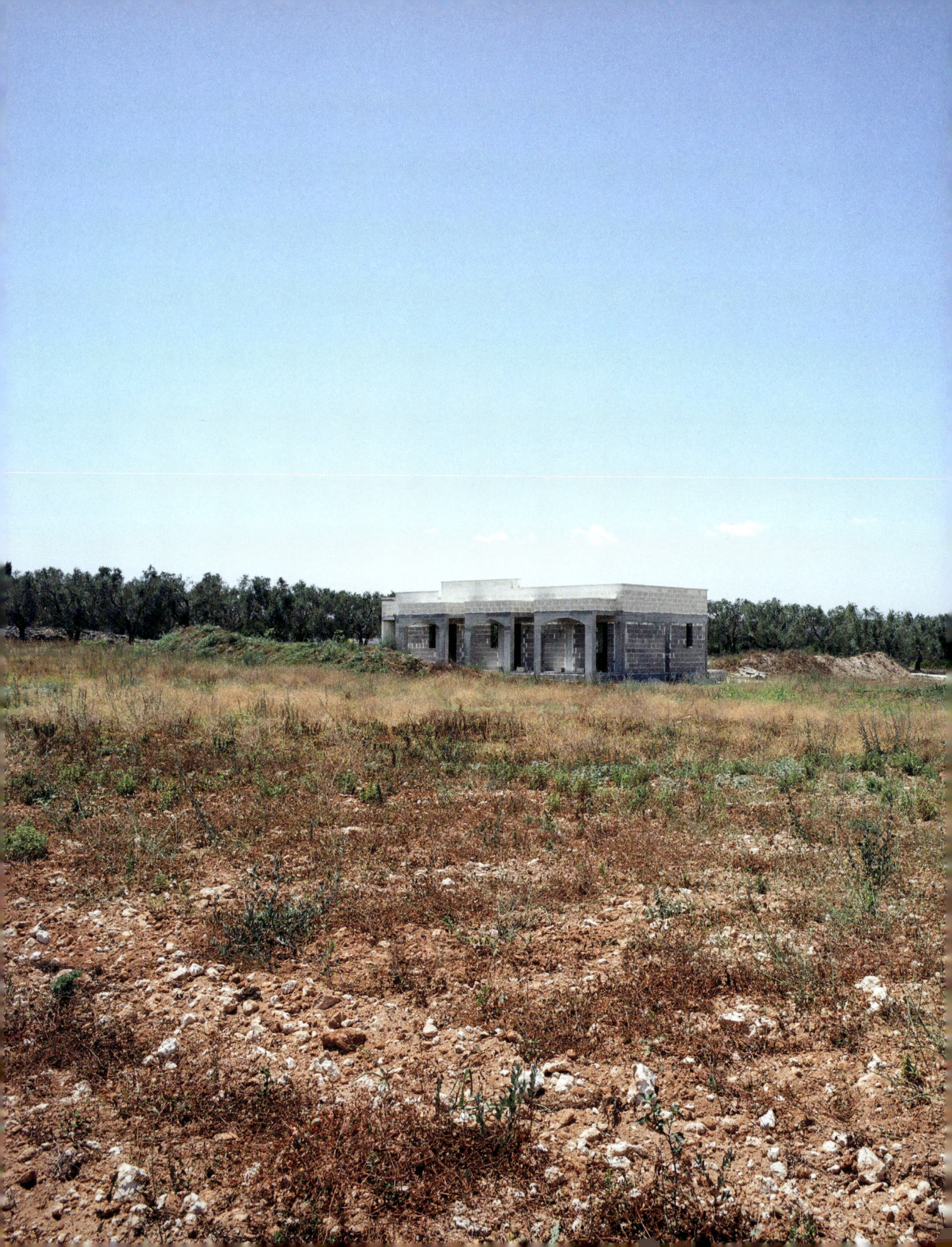

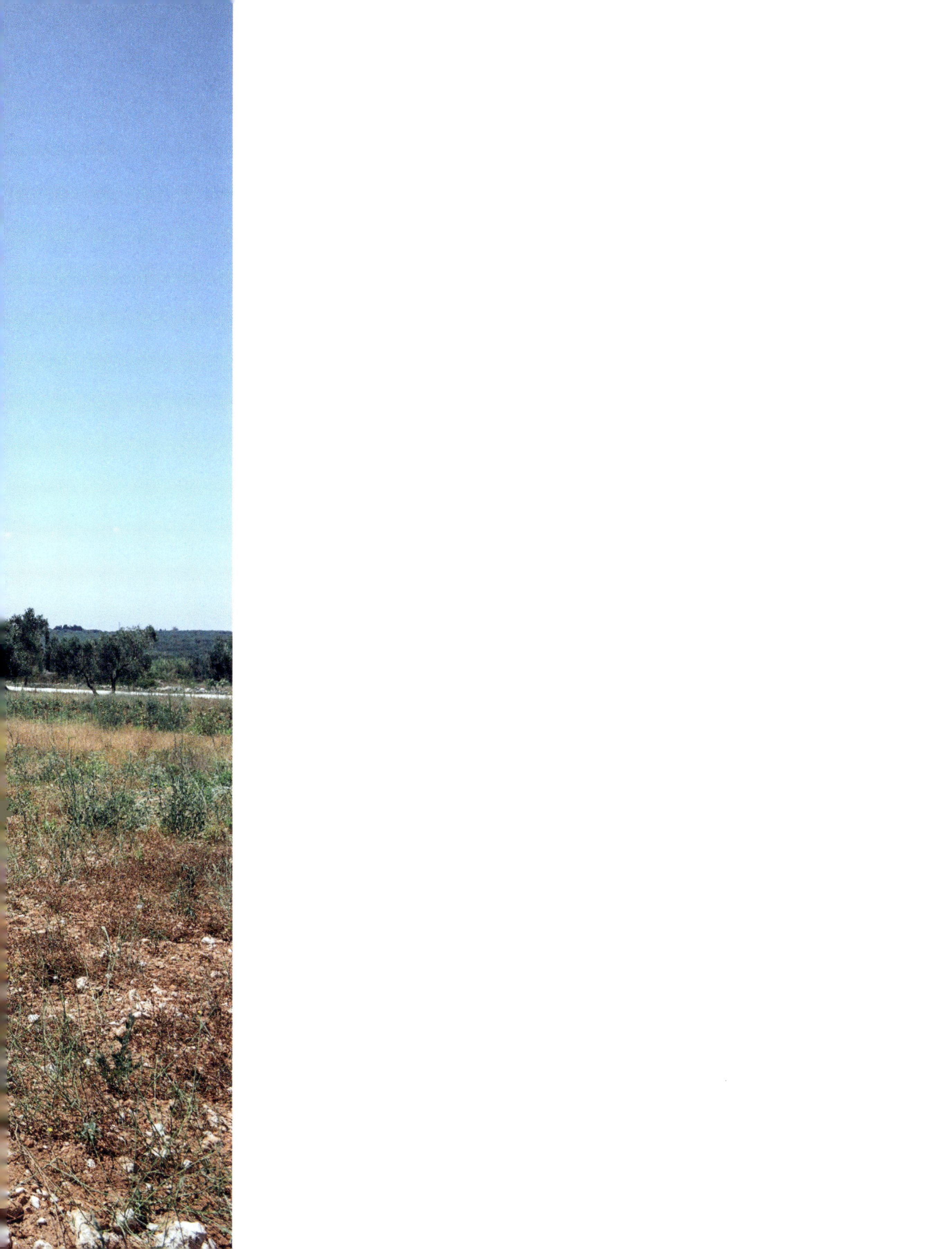

TERESA

Like with everyone else, the work on my house was interrupted, but we kept on going with our life's savings and when construction was finally complete and I was able to live in it with my family, the house became a source of pride for me and my husband, because all our sacrifices had been worth it. Now I am happy, because in the future, this house will go to my children!

Anch'io ho avuto i lavori della mia casa bloccati perché come tutti, si va avanti con i risparmi di una vita e, nel momento che si sono ultimati i lavori e sono potuta venire a viverci con la mia famiglia, questa casa è diventata una fonte di orgoglio per me e mio marito perché i nostri sacrifici hanno dato i propri frutti e sono felice perché un domani la casa andrà ai miei figli!

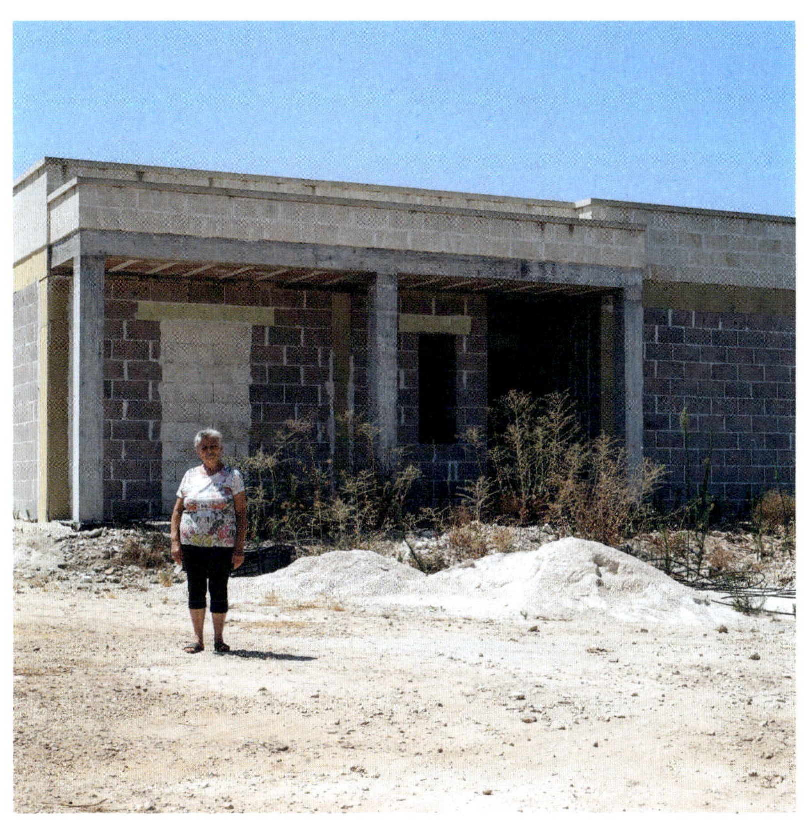

SPECCHIA GALLONE

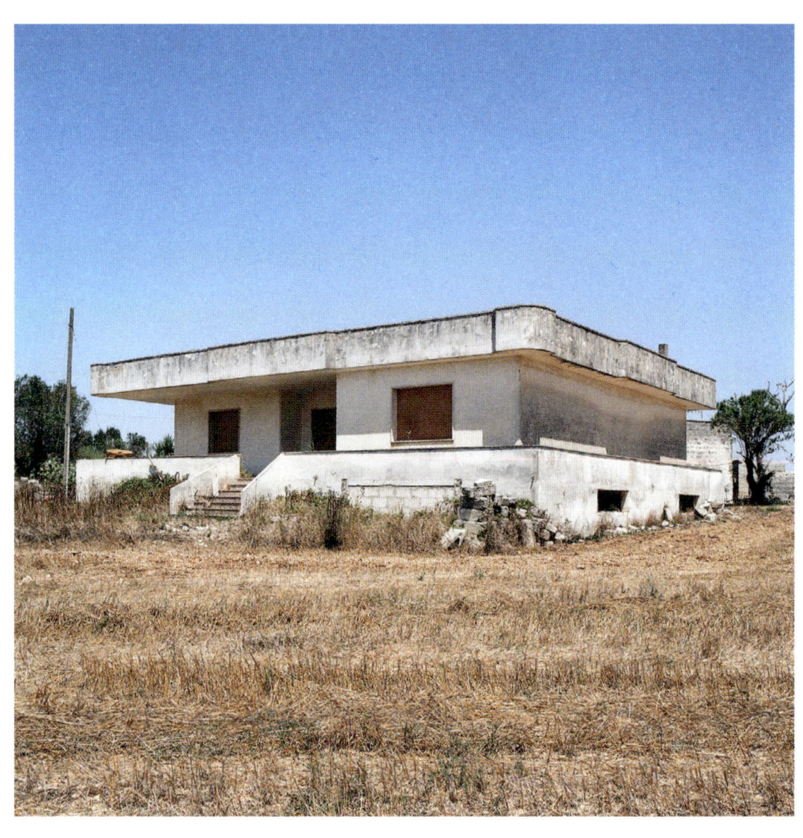

MINERVINO DI LECCE

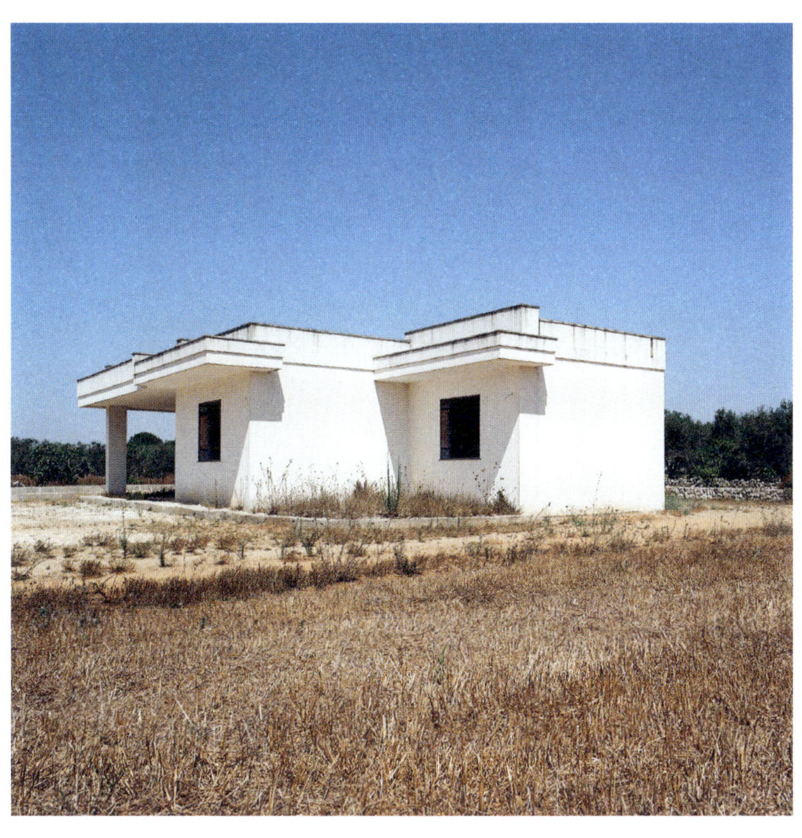

SPECCHIA GALLONE

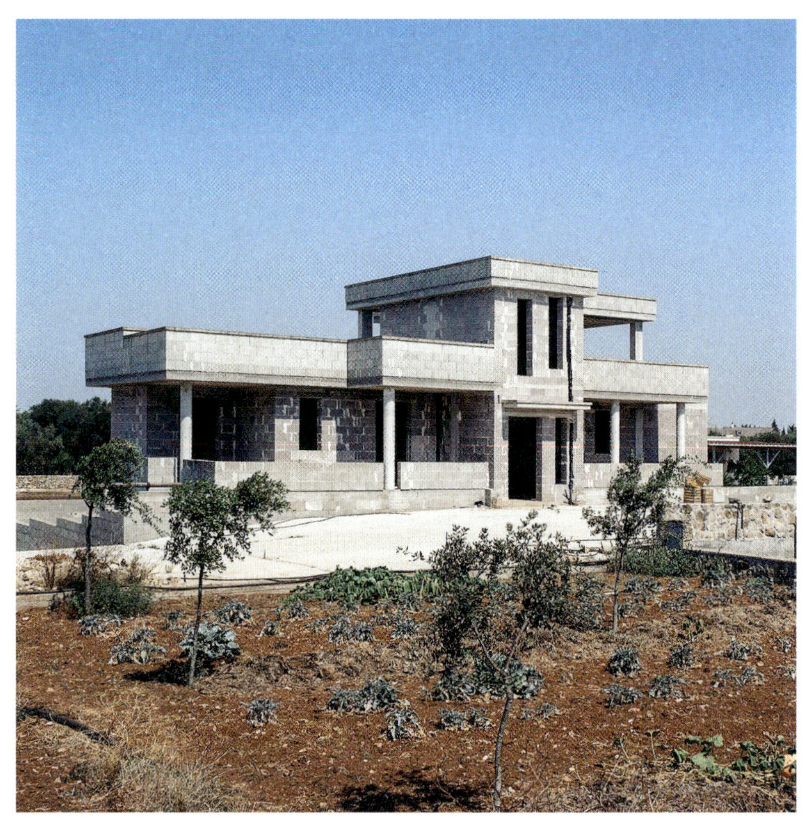

SOLETO

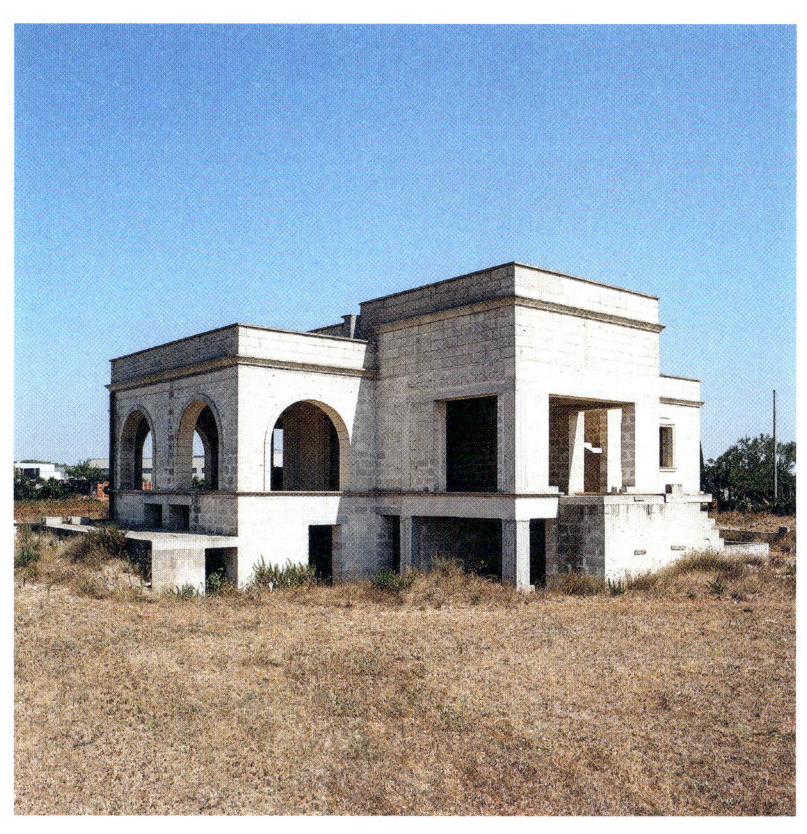

POGGIARDO

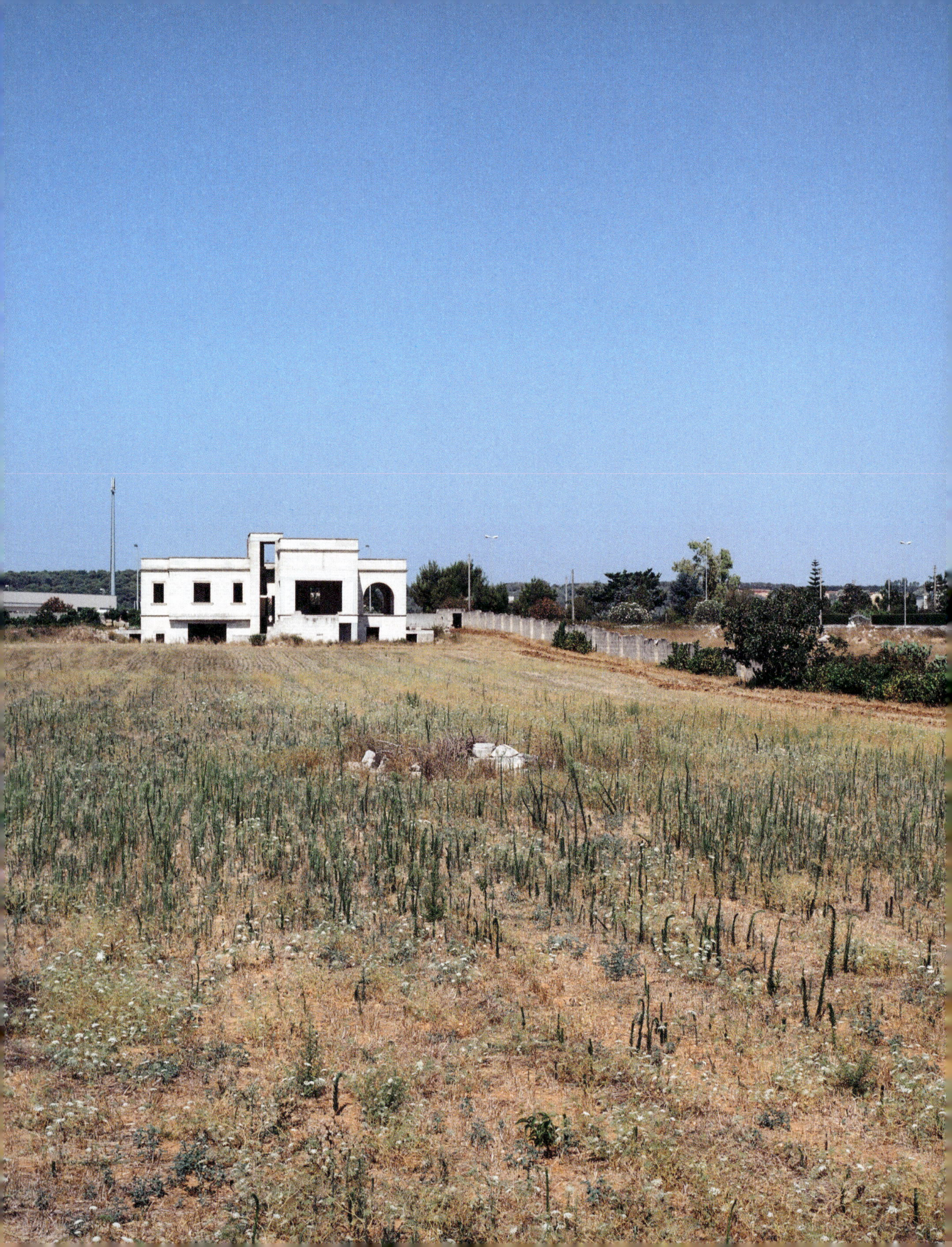

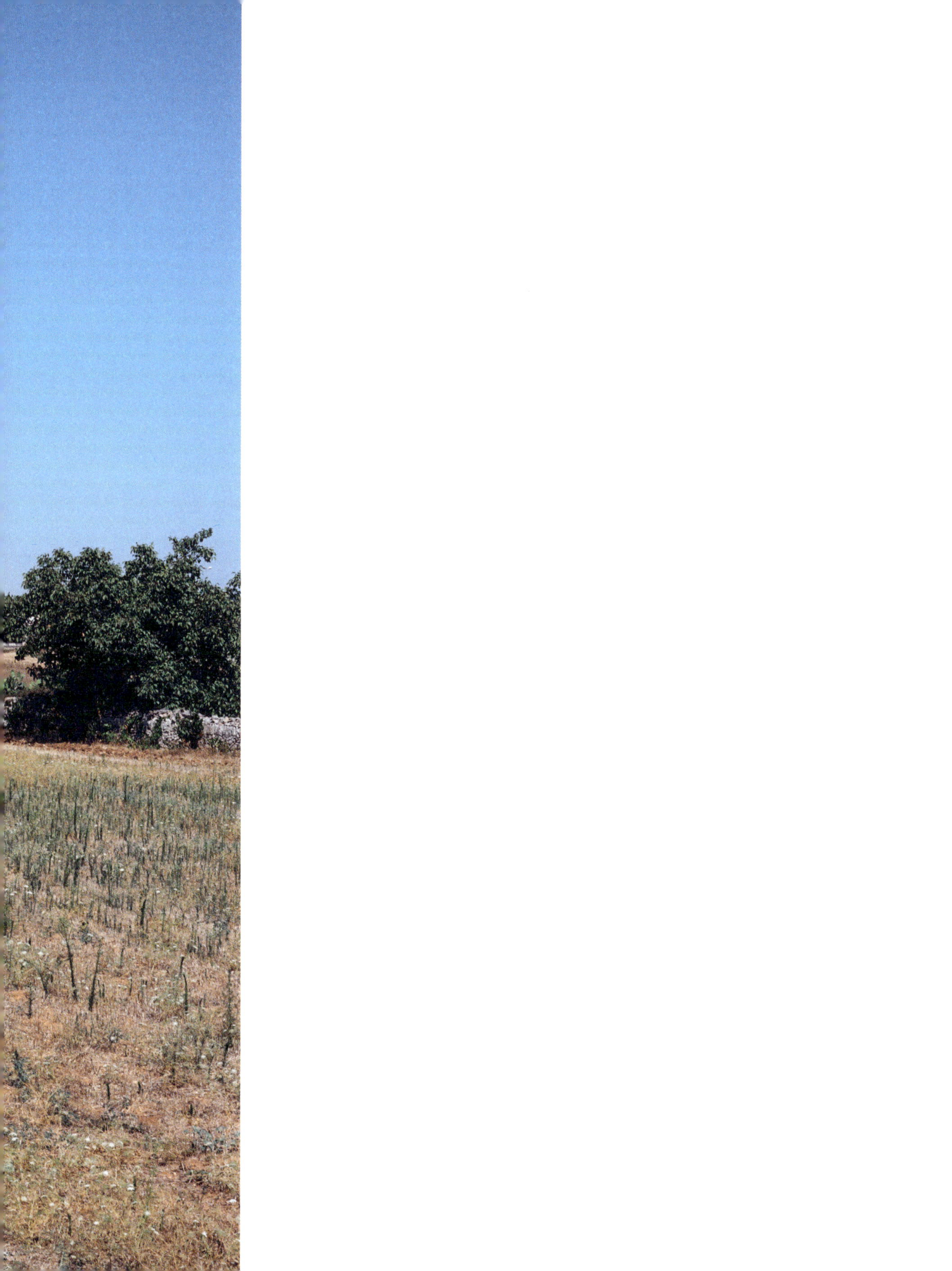

MARINA

Walking around these buildings, I see countless dreams and projects that have yet to be achieved. The unfinished work prevents them from being completed as desired. This is the way it is in Salento, where sacrifices become stones that, one after another, collect the bitter sweat and hopes of those who only wish to fulfill their life objectives.

————

Camminando intorno a questi edifici, vedo innumerevoli sogni e progetti ancora non realizzati. La mancanza di lavoro non consente di portarli a termine come desiderato. È così, che qui in Salento, i sacrifici diventano pietre che, una dopo l'altra, raccolgono il sudore amaro e la speranza di chi voleva solo portare a termine il suo obiettivo di vita.

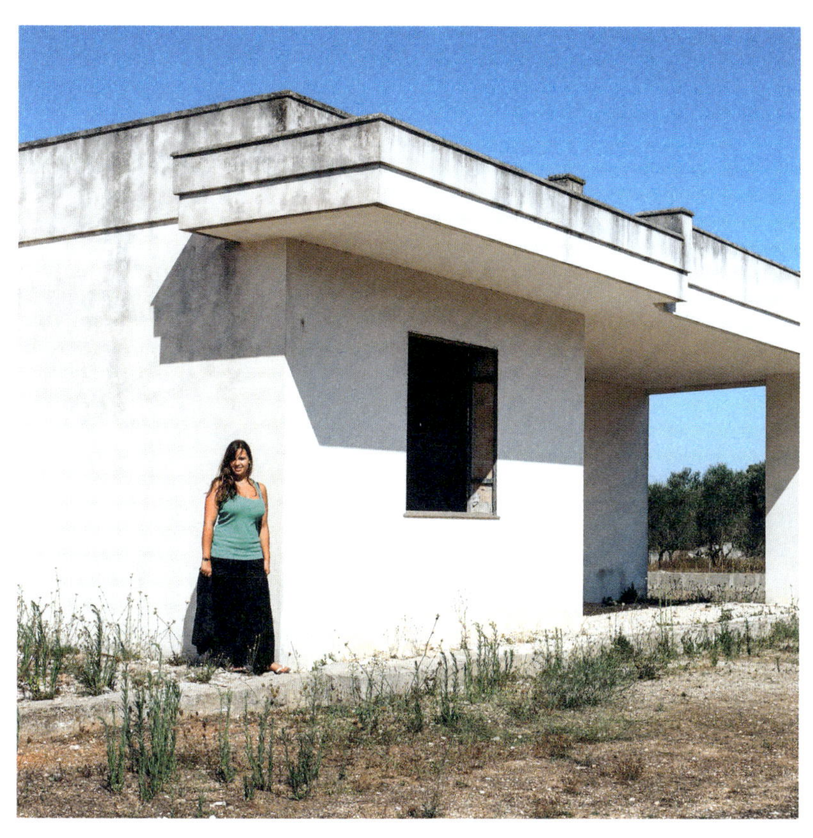

SPECCHIA GALLONE

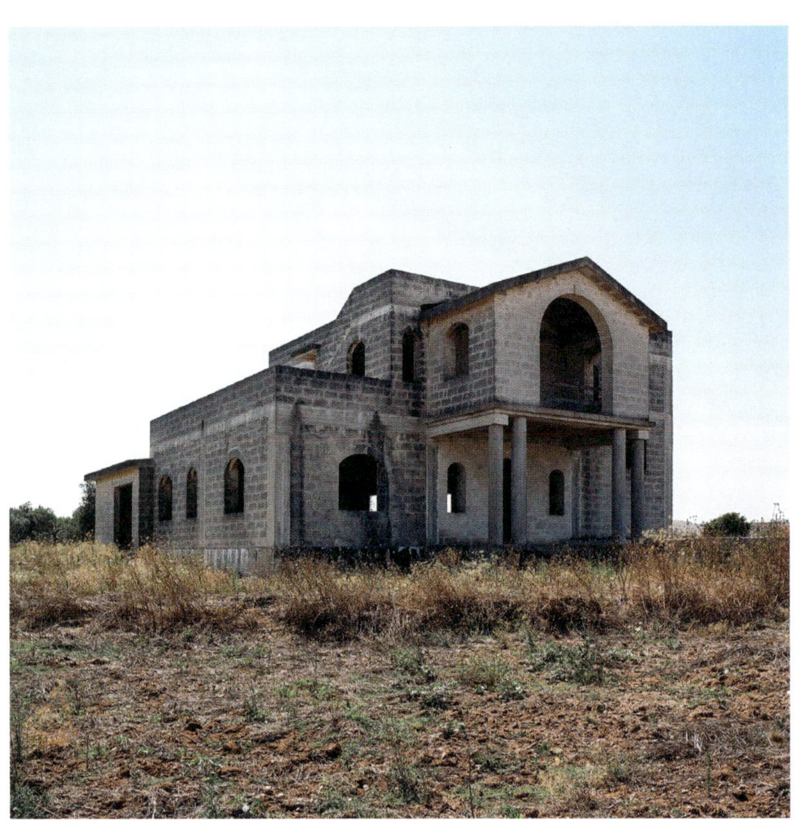

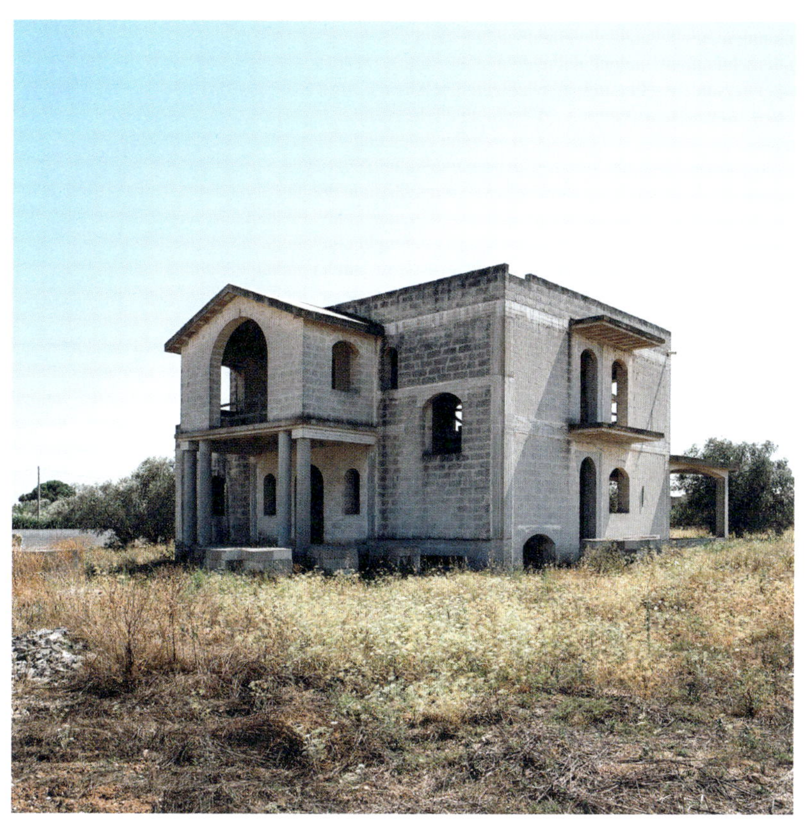

CANNOLE

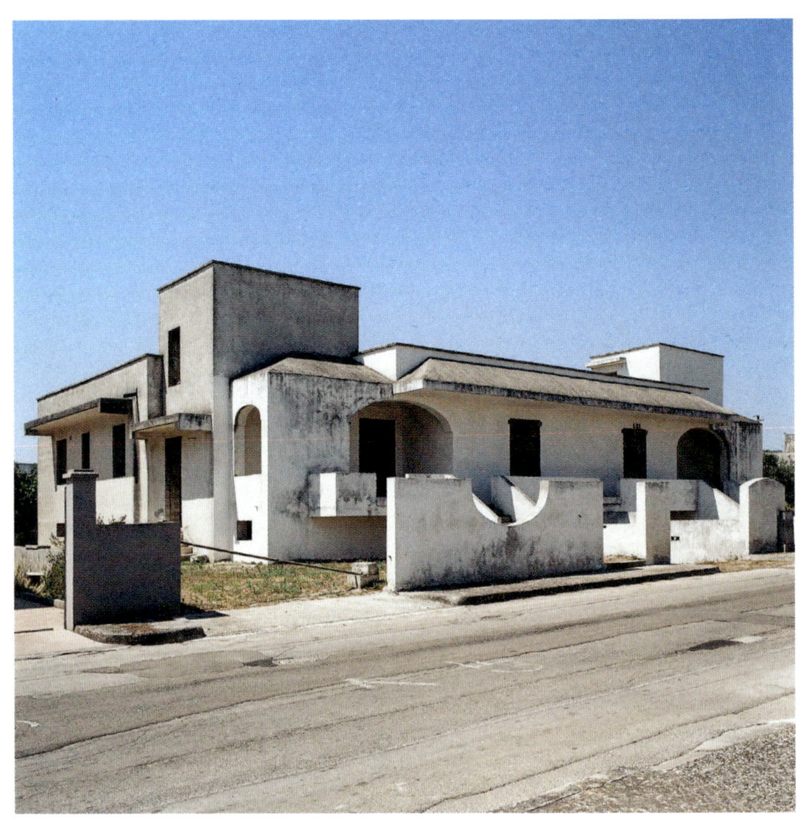

CERFIGNANO

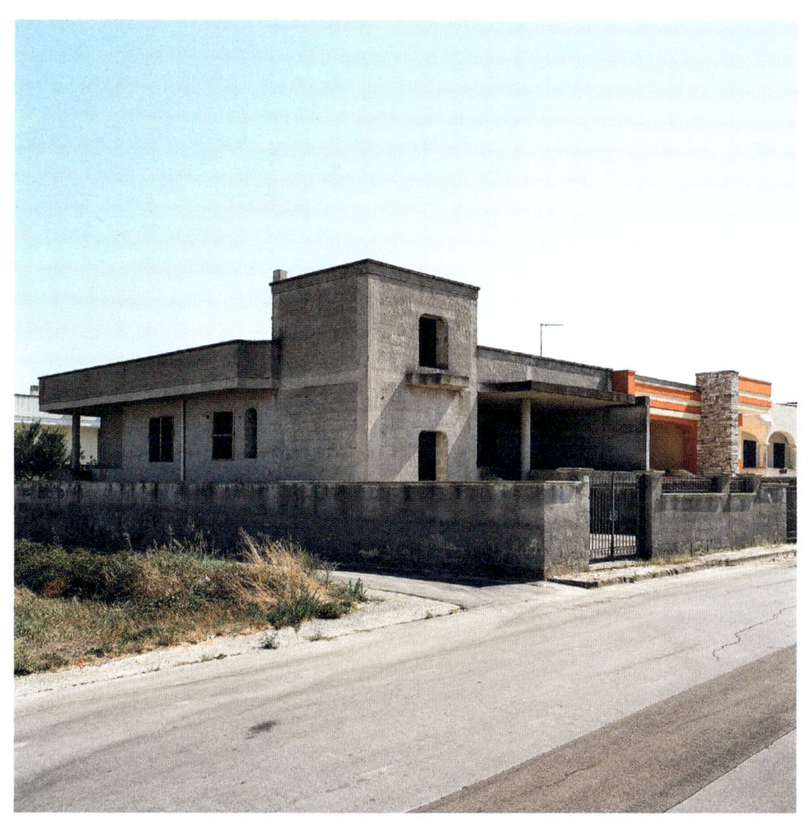

POGGIARDO

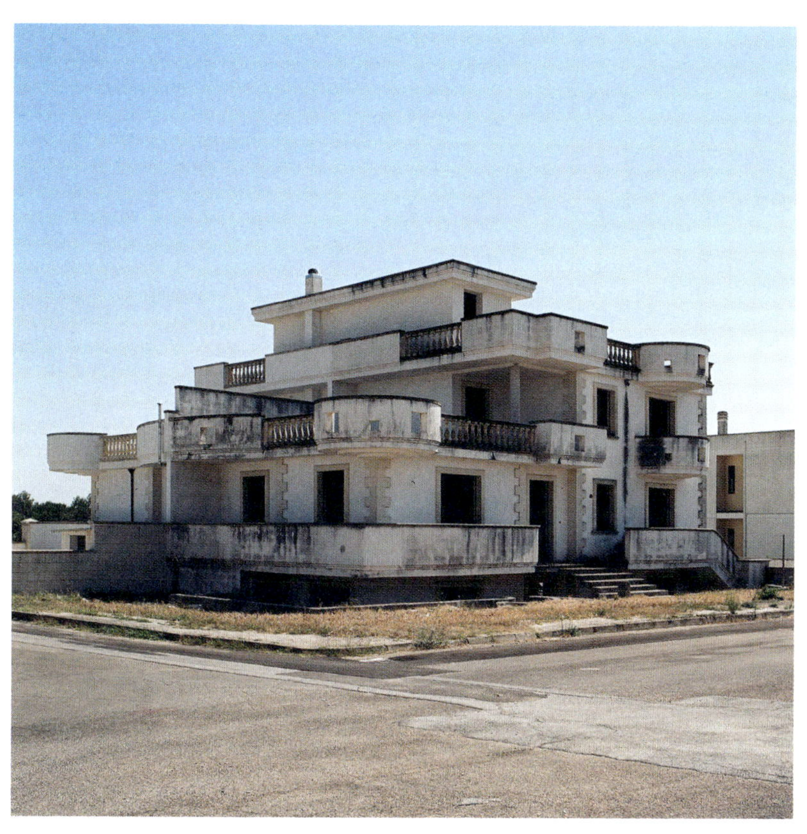

SANARICA

MARIA GRAZIA

There's a general consensus, as we all think more or less the same thing. These houses are sacrifices that parents have made for their children. Because of the crisis, it has been very difficult to finish constructing them. Before, most parents could gift their children a house. Today, many young people in the region have left to build their own future, and so the houses remain in this state. But for many, it is only temporary. Surely one day, they will be completed.

Diciamo che è un pensiero generale, pensiamo tutti più o meno la stessa cosa. Sono sacrifici che i genitori fanno per i propri figli. Solo che, ultimamente con la crisi è molto difficile completare i lavori. Prima un genitore riusciva maggiormente a dare in donazione una casa. Poi, al giorno d'oggi, molti giovani del posto sono fuori per costruire il proprio futuro. E quindi le case restano così. Ma molte di queste rimangono così temporaneamente. Sicuramente un giorno verranno portate a termine.

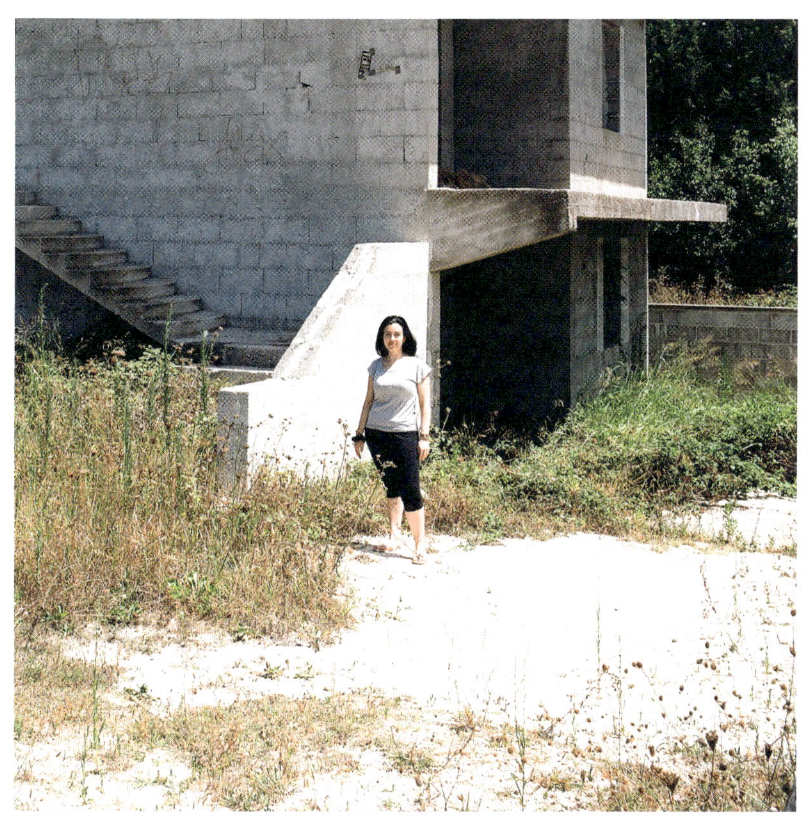

UGGIANO LA CHIESA

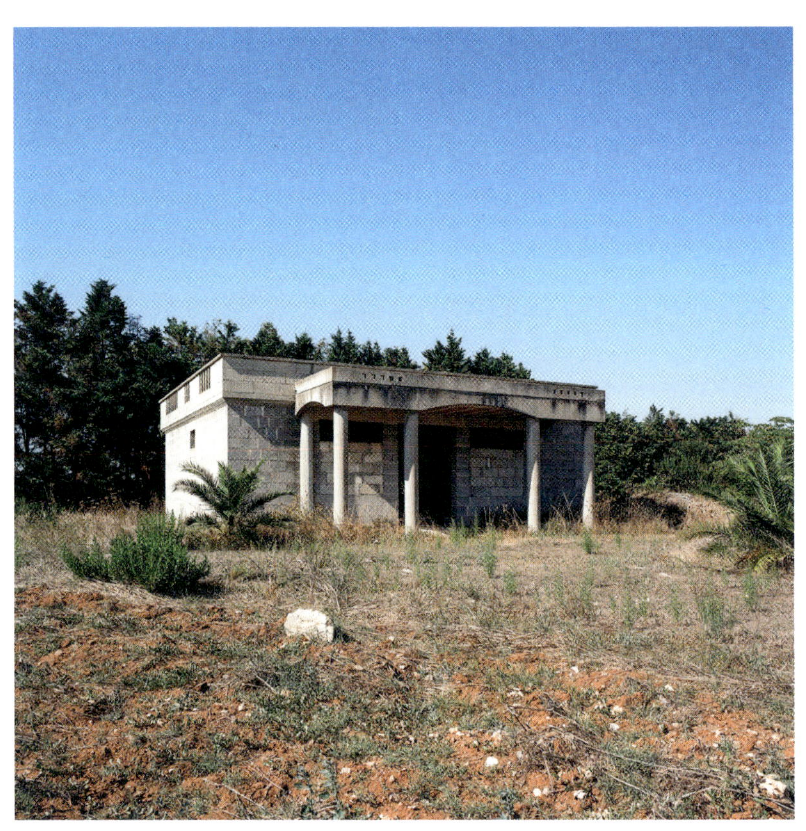

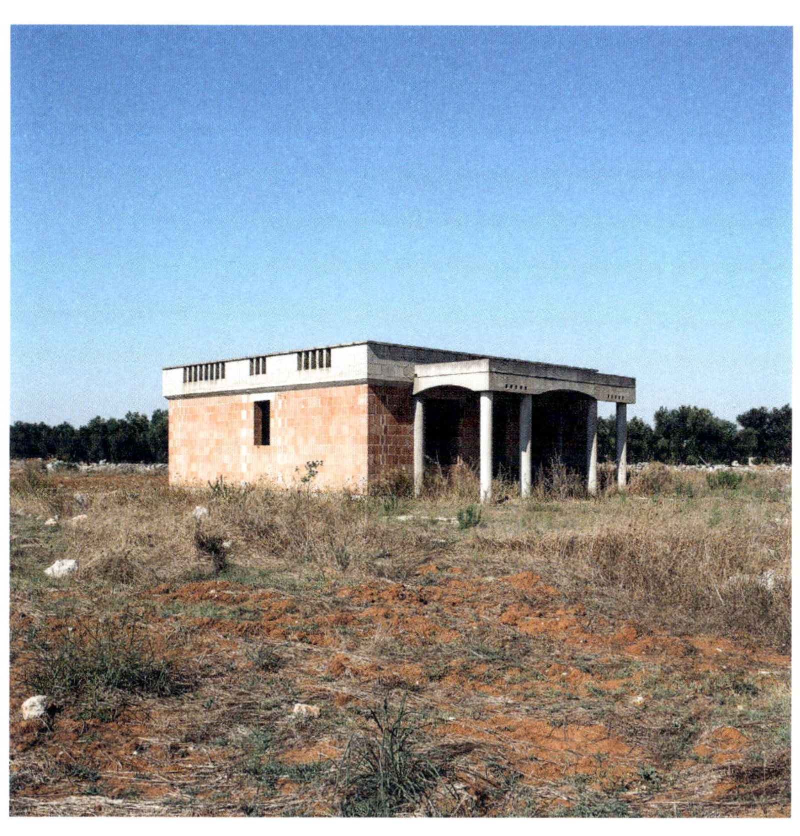

PALMARIGGI

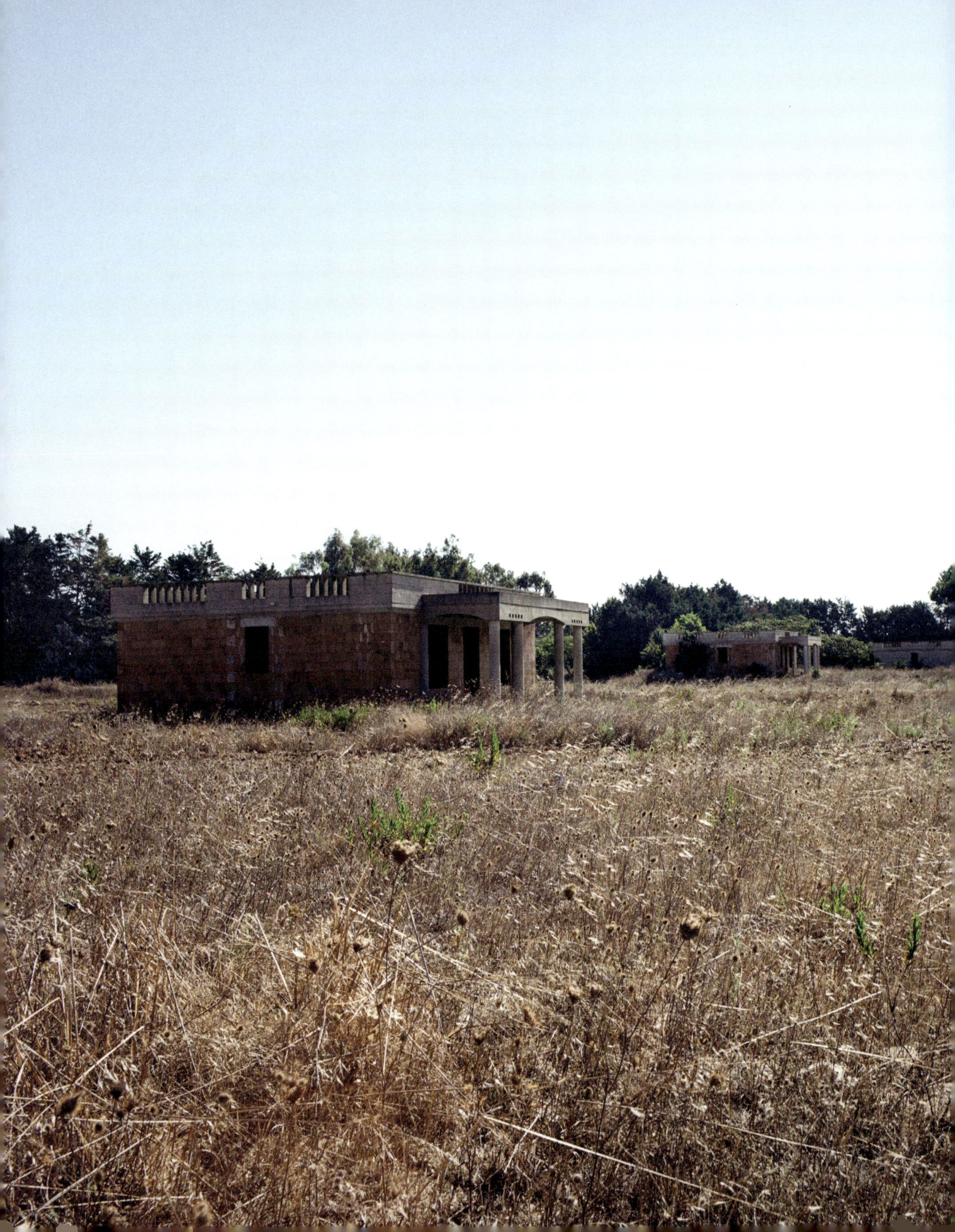

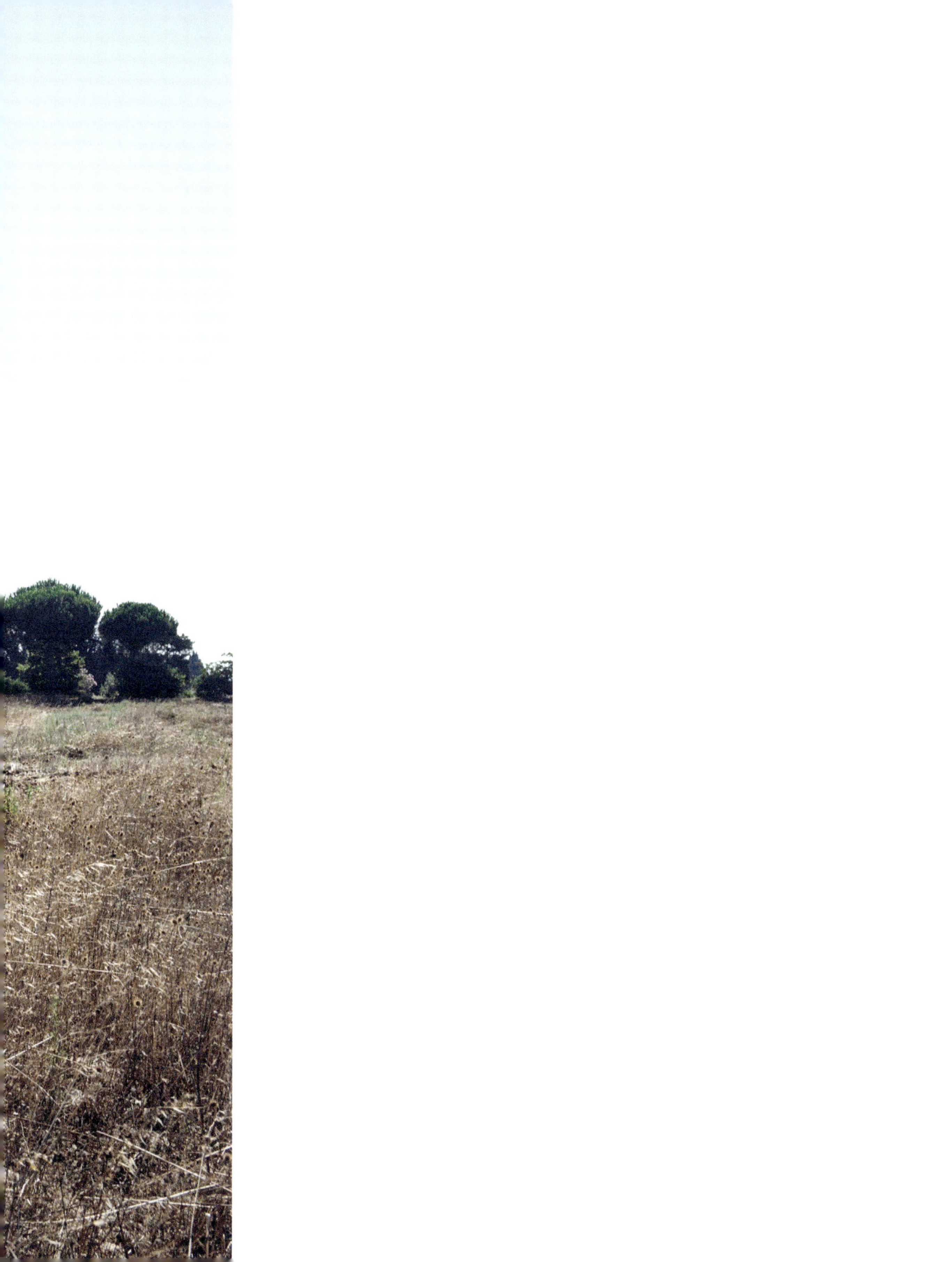

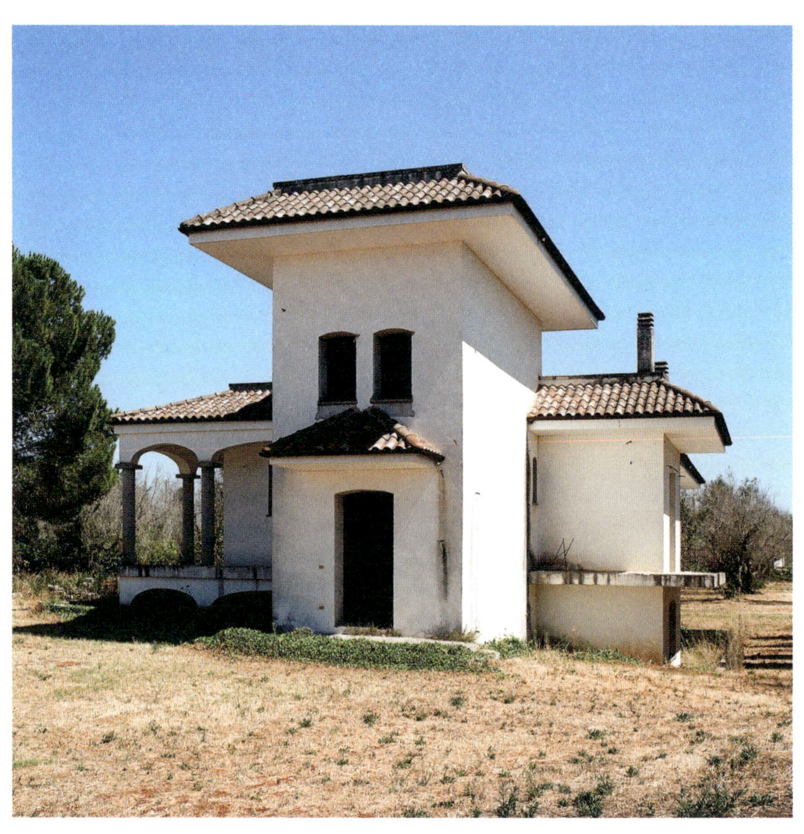

SAN CASSIANO

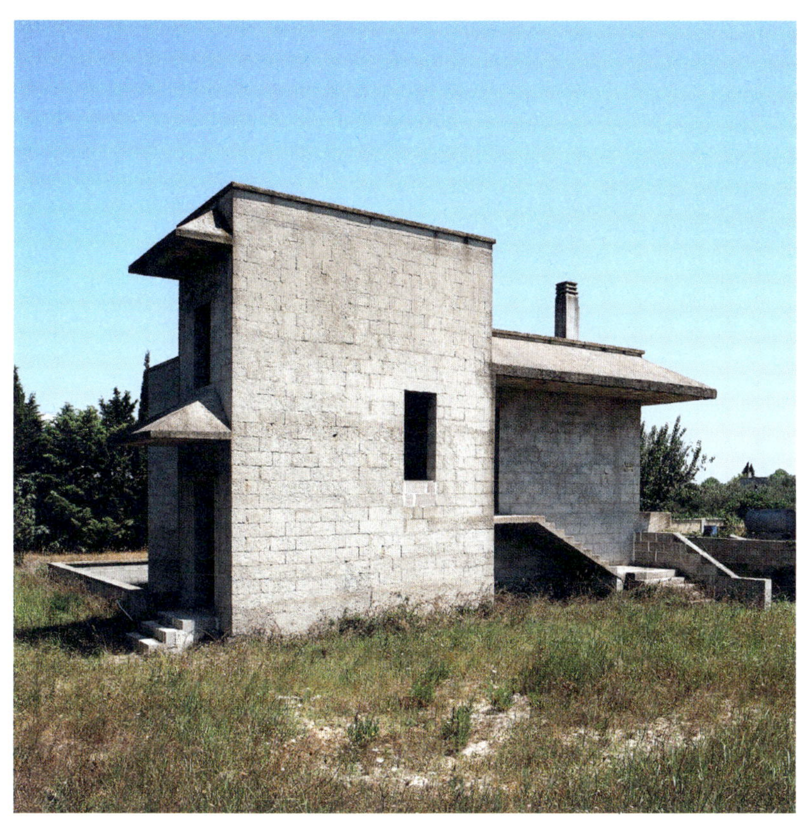

UGGIANO LA CHIESA

ANNA LISA

This house is really very beautiful and big, but has yet to be completed, which is common in Salento, evidently because it requires significant financial resources. Oftentimes, in order not to fall into debt, the owners wait for years to be able to scrape together enough to fulfill their own dreams!

———

Questa casa davvero molto bella e anche grande non risulta ancora completata, tipico del Salento, evidentemente perché occorrono importanti risorse finanziarie e molto spesso per non indebitarsi i proprietari aspettano anni per poter racimolare qualcosa in grado di realizzare i propri sogni!

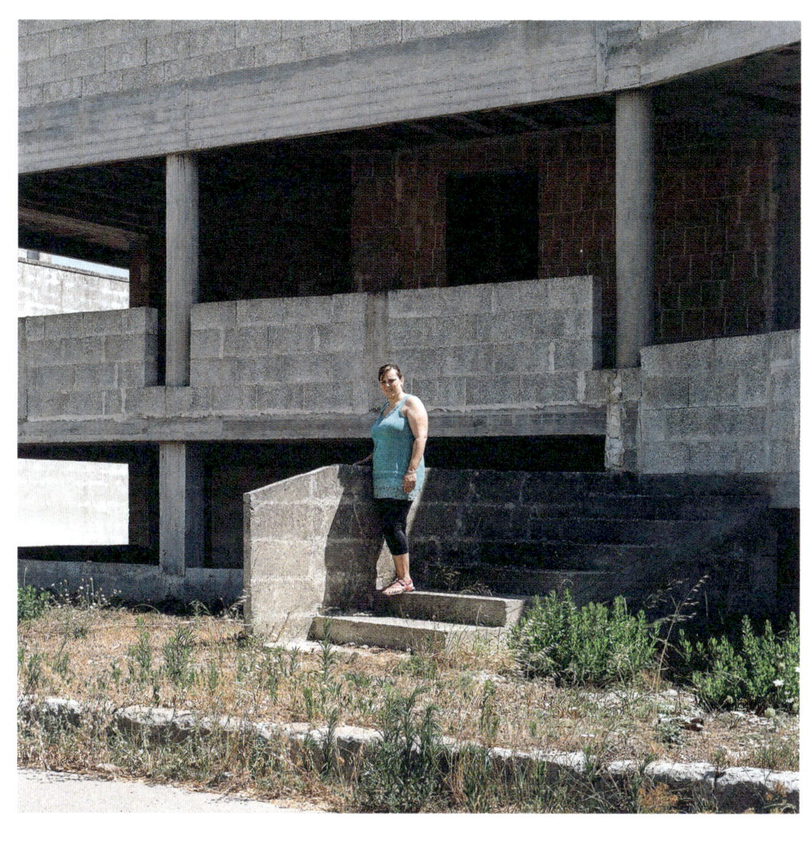

UGGIANO LA CHIESA

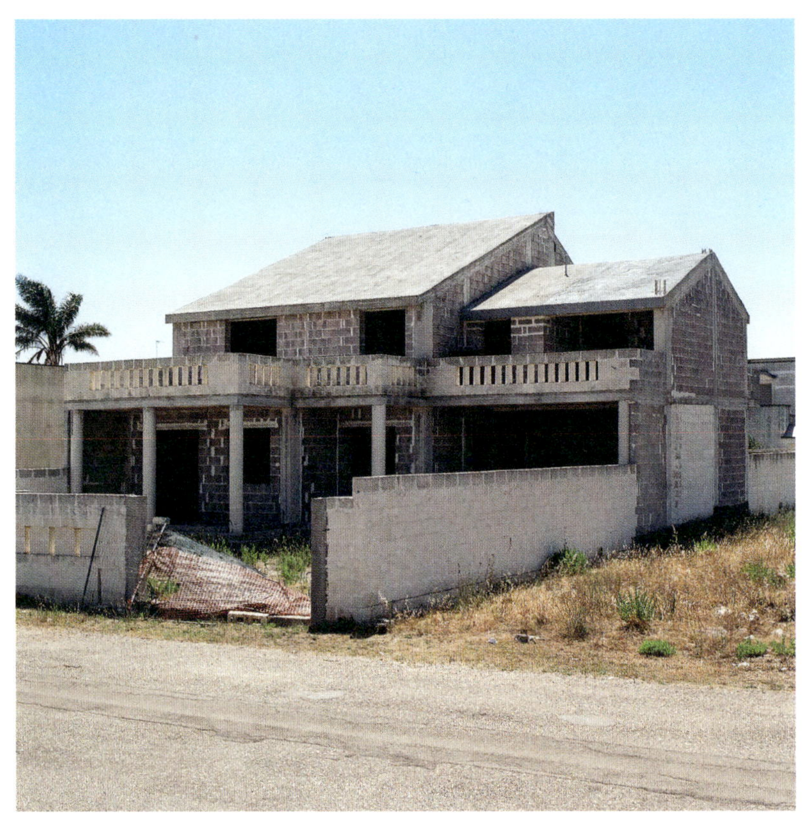

SCORRANO

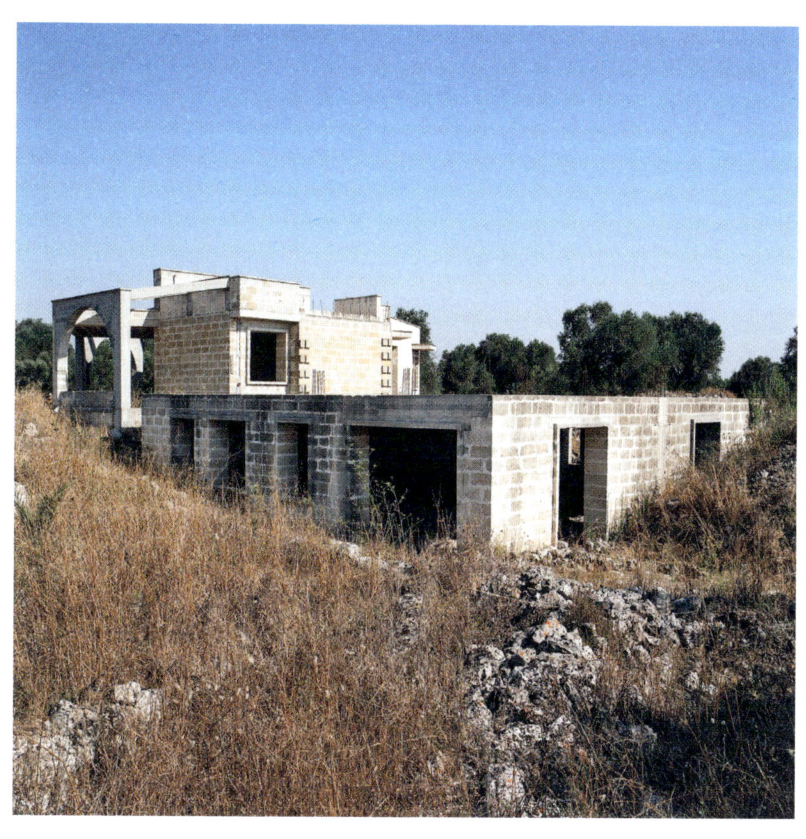

MURO LECCESE

DAVIDE AND OMAR

For us, these houses are a game. We have fun playing hide and seek inside them and exploring. But it's too bad, because such big houses could be used to build factories to give people work, or a nursery for little kids, or a nursing home for old people and other people in need!

Per noi rappresentano un gioco: ci divertiamo a giocarci dentro a nascondino o, a esplorarle. Bensì sono un peccato perché invece di case così grandi potrebbero costruire delle fabbriche per dare lavoro alla gente o un asilo nido per bambini piccoli o case di riposo per anziani e gente che ha bisogno!

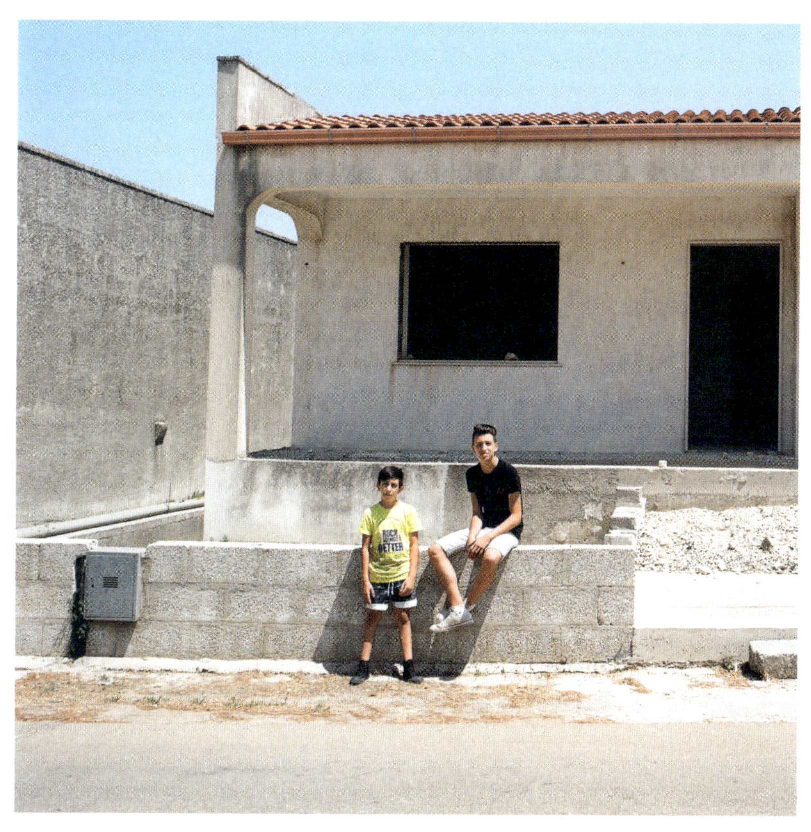

COCUMOLA

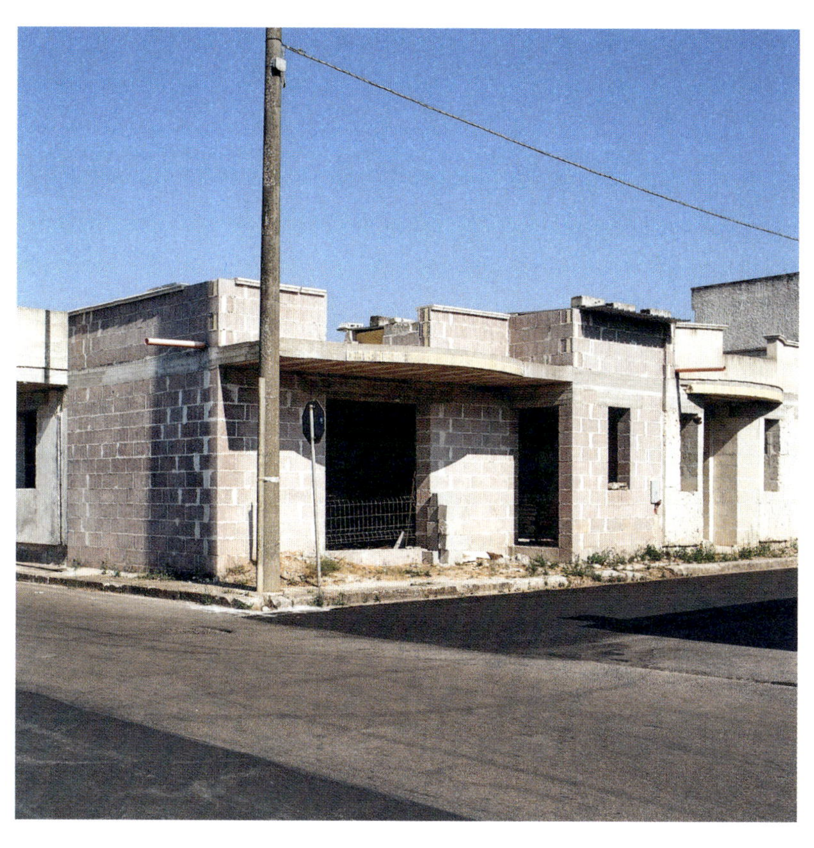

UGGIANO LA CHIESA

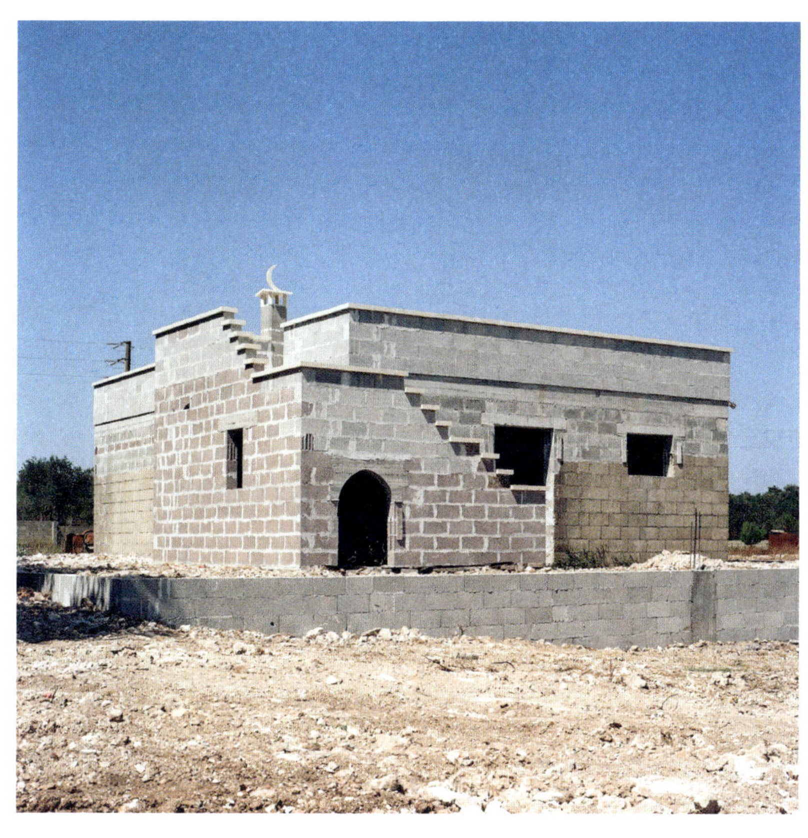

VITIGLIANO

STEVE

I'm originally from this area and I have always remained attached to my roots and to my region. That time of my life is still vivid in my memory and the sight of these unfinished houses gives me the impression that time came to a halt when I was a child. Just for an instant, I can jump back in time. The reality is probably very different for those who live in these little villages in the south of Italy.

Originario di questa regione, sono sempre rimasto legato alle mie radici e al mio paese. Oggi quel periodo è ancora molto presente nella mia memoria e la vista di queste case non finite mi dà l'impressione che il tempo si sia fermato a quando ero un bambino. Così, per un istante mi permette di fare un salto nel tempo. La realtà è sicuramente ben diversa per chi vive in questi piccoli borghi del sud Italia...

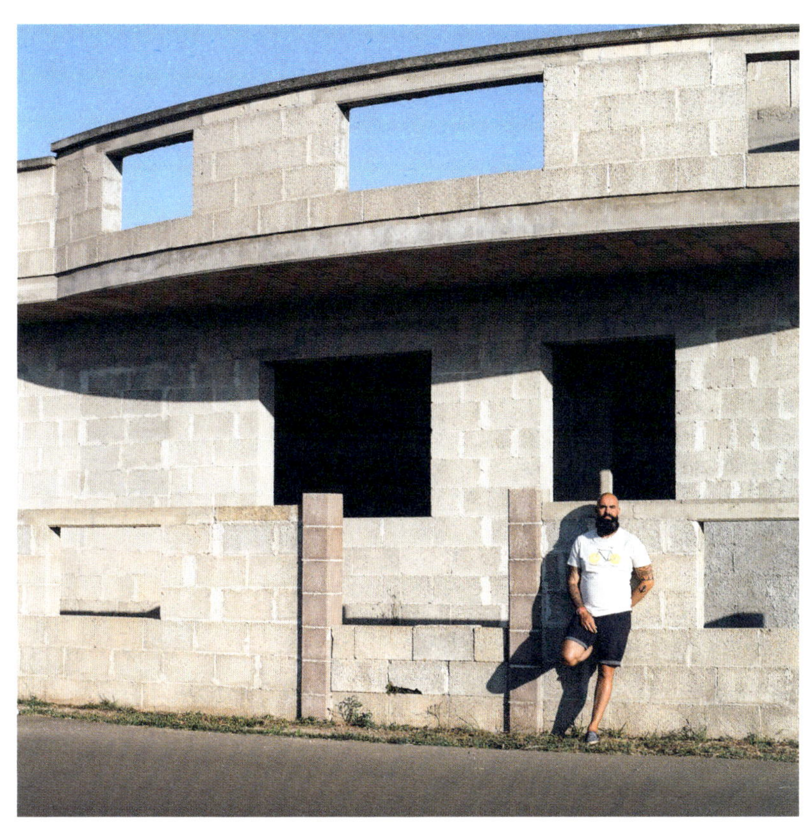

BARBARANO DEL CAPO

CONTEMPORARY LIVING IN SALENTO

Anna Bruna Menghini
Department of Civil, Constructional and Environmental Engineeering, Sapienza University of Rome

Only when understanding our place, we may be able to participate creatively and contribute to its history.
Christian Norberg-Schulz, *Genius Loci. Towards a Phenomenology of Architecture,* Rizzoli, New York, 1979

The houses featured in Gabriel Mauron's photos appear at first glance to be a repertoire of examples of the common practice of illegal or semi-illegal construction on Italian territory that is particularly prevalent in the South. However, if we look closely, these images prompt us to make observations on different levels, from the anthropological-cultural and socio-economic, to the more strictly architectural and urbanistic, leading us to reflect on the existential fundamentals of "living" (Heidegger).

If we exclude speculative operations, a large proportion of this widespread development in contemporary outskirts and suburban areas is made up of single-family houses that have been built by the future inhabitants for their own needs. They are often emigrants who plan to return to their homeland in the future and live in their region of origin. These constructions are carried out slowly and with much patience, using savings that have been laboriously earned elsewhere and proudly invested in their homeland. However, they often remain unfinished due to a lack of funds, or evolving family needs.

These houses can are almost be viewed in their universality as "monuments of emigration". They have been designed with the best intentions and with particular care, and endeavor to be tributes to the land of origin, placing themselves in the ideal continuity of the secular work carried out by the forefathers when constructing on the territory. Why then do these houses appear to be in such dissonance with their context and so full of formal errors?

"Why do all architects, good or bad, end up spoiling the lake?" wondered Adolf Loos at the beginning of the twentieth century. "The farmer doesn't. (...) The architect, like almost every inhabitant of the city, has no civilization. He lacks the security of the peasant, who instead has his own civilization. The inhabitant of the city is an uprooted man." Loos believed in the permanence of a "civilization of living", in other words, "that inner and outer balance of man guaranteed only by rational thought and action", and trusted in the ability of the inhabitant who is "not uprooted" to correctly orient his choices in "being in the world"; Heinrich Tessenow was able to practice an "architecture of modesty" as a modern man; Giuseppe Pagano and Bernard Rudofsky viewed "architecture without architects" as a means of renewal through a heartfelt return to one's origins. But what has become of all this?

The shared culture of living, the survival of its rituals and forms, the process that guaranteed the spontaneous transfer of "know-how", as well as its evolution, have entered a crisis in the modern era, due to socio-economic changes. As a result, the patrician villa and rural house have declined, while the phenomenon of isolated suburban "cottages" designed for the comfort and representation of the lower middle classes has spread, following the Anglo-Saxon model of the "garden city" (Menghini 2007). The disconnect between working and living has deprived the house of its relationship with the territory and the productive landscape – a relationship exemplified by Veneto's "villa with barchessa", Pianura Padana's "cascina" and the Apulian "masseria". These forms of aristocratic and peasant living have been adapted to the lifestyle of the middle class. At the same time, the bourgeois villa has taken on the stylistic features of noble palaces and courtly architecture (just as Palladio introduced the architecture of the *pronaos* temple into domestic architecture), and extrapolated upon the morphemes and ornamental elements that traditionally ennobled the rural architecture of large estates.

This transfer of forms and symbols is all the more accentuated in the contemporary world, with the staging of a theatricality of living that must be invented. The Post-Modern movement played a decisive role in recovering historical and vernacular forms through pop culture, favouring their circulation through diverse forms of mass media. Today, the aristocratic ways of living that are typical of the parvenu and the *clichés* of Hollywood luxury manifest themselves in an inexpensive version. An inhabitant affirms their individuality – the condition of being uprooted, and having lost their status as a peasant, an aristocrat or even a metropolitan citizen – and the social status they have achieved, which prevail over the quest for a simple and authentic way of life, and the development of an organic relationship with the land and one's fellow human beings.

In this sense, Adolf Loos's statements seem all the more relevant today. He has reflected a great deal on the crisis of living in modern times, the relationship between a house and the place upon which it stands, its inherited culture and the desires of the inhabitant, as well as the role of the architect in designing of the house. From modernity onwards, the necessity of having a "project" to construct a house – a practice derived from loosening ties with the traditional way of living and the construction profession, and in the passage from traditional craftsmanship to the industrial field of construction – has become critical. Even satisfying the most immediate and basic necessities, like the need to live, must now be the result of a project, and therefore a choice. In a world where all forms are presented as equals and are ready to be used completely freely, the possibilities are endless.

These houses are the result of a process in which the designer - whether architect, surveyor or engineer – has responded to the wishes and financial situation of the client, offering only their technical skills and rarely succeeding in orienting the taste of the future inhabitants. It is almost as if we are witnessing a reversal of the slogan "architecture without architects" to "architects without architecture", which is to say, architects without roots or disciplinary guarantees.

The development of the model of the isolated, single-family house that is cheaply built or self-constructed is a phenomenon that extends to most of the regions facing the Mediterranean. In the Balkans, for example, this problem has been growing since the end of the twentieth century due to socio-political changes, but the sense of belonging is more complicated, as these places have complex stratified identities (Menghini 2016). Here, like elsewhere, architectural forms appear to be simulacra imported from Western culture or freely taken from the traditional repertoire. While Giuseppe Pagano pointed to the rationality of "minor architecture" and the functionality of forms produced by material culture, thereby providing justification as to why they continue to be revisited, these forms have now become unconscious post-modern citations. There is no shared language, no rigor of compositional grammars, no rationality of use. The new techniques increase compositional freedom and loosen the principles of congruence between material, structure, form, spaces and language. But in spite of all this, the melodies of ancient songs continue to echo in the houses of these "emigrants of the spirit". The original architectural forms that were glimpsed in a distant time and nostalgically preserved in memory have finally been brought back home.

In addition to an ambiguity in building type and architectural language, these houses also highlight how the logic that governed urban and rural settlements in the past has been transformed. Some of them are isolated in the countryside, while others are aggregated in the low-density fabric of the "widespread periphery", unable to communicate with their surroundings or the adjacent houses, searching for an originality that results in a kind of Esperanto. Rather than tuning in to their contexts, these peripheral and suburban areas often develop through the invention or reenactment of an ideal. The Palladian villa, Apulian farmhouse, Hollywood villa, fairy house and Nordic castle all blend to form a potpourri that is incapable of creating an urban or rural "landscape", despite its hyperreal physicality.

Nevertheless, in the examples selected for this volume, we can still identify clear references to the Salento way of living. In terms of building type we can recognize the residue of images that have been engrained in memory, such as the *masserie* (farmhouses). A clear desire for form is expressed through the articulation of the bodies of these buildings, the care with which the grounding connection and openings have been installed, as well as the choice of material and decorative features. Elements of houses of the Apulian tradition are rekindled: turrets, entrance stairs, porticos and loggias, and rusticated cantonals. Contemporary customs, such as balconies and roofs with offset pitches, which have no place in tradition, are intercepted and filtered through the imagination of local culture.

As for the language of construction, the massive character of continuous masonry that defines Mediterranean culture is preserved. Although these houses may be unfinished, they are not naked skeletons; instead, they reveal structures in which reinforced concrete and masonry work together to mimic and preserve the traits of continuous and massive constructions. The framed structure, which is deemed to be more economically advantageous and technically efficient, has been adapted to the image of the masonry house, but the overhang of the balconies and unusual shape of the porticoes denounce the concrete structure.

Plaster and stone are united in these buildings, replicating a dialogue that characterizes Apulian cities on a smaller scale, with the noble parts in stone standing out from the plastered body of the building. Precious materials, such as local stone, are often used as a simple covering. However, the themes addressed by modern architecture, from Semper's "theory of cladding" to Le Corbusier's research into "domino" structures, have not been disseminated and remain the heritage of *élite* culture.

The photographer focuses on the unfinished condition of these houses. The constructional reality is that the unfinished is more unsettling in the present than the past; while ancient ruins reveal the soul of a building and represent "a part of the whole", the incompleteness of reinforced concrete buildings are perceived as a shortcoming, mercilessly revealing the "ruse" of the prosthesis that supports the architectural form.

If we carefully examine the photographed houses, their poetry transpires above all through their suspension in space and time. These "young" dwellings are still naked and defenseless, but have already aged before living and being lived in, their black holes like lidless eyes that remain wide open, resting on harsh, barren ground that may never produce a garden. The metaphysical suspension lends these constructions a certain nobility, as well as a surreal presence.

In these un-situated and un-situating spaces, we can feel the absence of daily life and "bodies" that give rise to the condition of "living" (Vitta), like the staging of a domestic life that is imagined but never achieved. In this prolonged state of incompleteness, they almost seem to be houses of the soul rather than the body, the materialization of an unfulfilled dream where imagination, ambition, desire and aspiration, combined with regret and nostalgia reign. We can imagine endless life projects, tales of individuals and families that have grown, been divided, and then later reunited. If we follow in the footsteps of these suspended dreams, an epic emerges – one that may no longer be prevalent in Europe, but can be found in developing countries that have high rates of emigration. These dreams are fragile because they are not firmly rooted in the culture of living or the economy of the territories. The slightest change in economic or social circumstances is enough to make these houses superfluous, like the wreckage of lost ships. In the current economic crisis, these houses are increasingly transformed from a dream into a nightmare for the family that has to maintain them and the community that is obliged to adopt them.

The photographer's precious work does not only focus on the universal and shared dimension of living, but seeks to understand, rather than denounce, and to observe reality with intelligence and engagement. If the house is not only the expression of a need, but also manifests, even involuntarily, an aesthetic, representative and symbolic dimension, and if the aim is to not only create a useful and functional space, but also an object that is capable of making its mark on the territory through its presence, then it does not only belong to the owner, but also the inhabitants of the area, its strength residing in its external facies.

As the photographer is conscious that the house cannot exist without the presence of man, who is both the unit of measure and the interpreter of space, he portrays people next to each house. The photos do not predictably associate the buildings with those who own them, but instead feature those who regularly frequent the places marked by these presences, those who were born there, but now live far away, and the occasional passers-by.

The photographer does not only capture images, but probes the attitudes and opinions of those who cohabit with these architectural objects, who appropriate their exterior appearance with a quick glance, and who play next to them, violating their intimacy. In the presence of this "protagonist" who arouses admiration, curiosity, annoyance and reproach, there are some who desire them by identifying with their owners, others who observe them with poeticism and still others who question or are critical of them, denouncing their wastefulness and uselessness.

By involving the point of view of those who perceive the object of living from the outside, the photographer highlights its public, collective and social significance. He seeks to relate the impressions of those who have observed over time the transformation and occupation of an open space in the countryside, a plot of nature, or an urban void, who now experience these places as they remain suspended in a limbo between the public and the private spheres, but still display a willingness to expose themselves without defenses or locks.

The photos do not reveal the interior spaces, but we can easily imagine rooms that are deliberately oversized, cold and incongruous, designed to flaunt prosperity and opulence rather than for the comfort of living. Needs that were real and authentic in the past are now dominated by the stereotypes of mass society. Today's middle class dreams of being liberated from the apartment – a symbol of the "uniformity" of housing – in order to possess an independent house where one can live freely and convert a plot of nature into a "mournful garden". They are employees, industrial workers and peasants who seek an identity of their own in the "widespread suburbs" and peri-urban countryside (Trevisan). Due to the globalization brought about by television clichés, we are increasingly confronted with these villas of desire, loneliness and terror that are scattered all over the Italian territory, each of them different and yet all the same.

Gabriel Mauron's images offer us the opportunity to deliver ourselves from this condition. They communicate a sentiment of bewilderment and permanent transience that surround these artifacts that have been abandoned under the meridian sun. At the same time, they capture a moment of life produced by those who animate these places with a glance and a fleeting thought.

Works cited

Heidegger, Martin. "Bauen Wohnen Denken", 1951.

Loos, Adolf. "Architektur" (1910). *Trotzdem.* 1900-1930, Innsbruck, Brenner-Verlag, 1931.

Menghini, Anna Bruna. "Unfinished houses in Albanian landscape." *Evoked. Architectural diptychs,* edited by Domenico Pastore. Bari, Giuseppe Laterza, 2016, pp. 19-23.

Menghini, Anna Bruna. "Abitare e costruire: la ricerca teorica sullo spazio domestico nel moderno." *La casa dei maestri. L'architettura domestica nel Movimento Moderno,* edited by Michele Beccu and Loredana Ficarelli. Bari, Mario Adda Editore, 2007, pp. 91-108.

Pagano, Giuseppe and Guarniero Daniel. *Architettura rurale italiana.* Milan, 1936.

Rudofsky, Bernard. *Architecture without architects: a short introduction to non-pedigreed architecture.* New York, Museum of Modern Art, 1964.

Tessenow, Heinrich. *Hausbau und dergleichen,* Berlin, Bruno Cassirer, 1916.

Trevisan, Vitaliano. *Tristissimi giardini,* Rome and Bari, Laterza, 2010.

Vitta, Maurizio. *Dell'abitare. Corpi, spazi, oggetti, immagini.* Turin, Piccola Biblioteca Einaudi, 2008

SERGIO

People have money problems and can only invest little by little. Everyone is free to do as they wish.

La gente ha problemi di soldi e investe poco a poco. Ognuno è libero di fare quello che vuole.

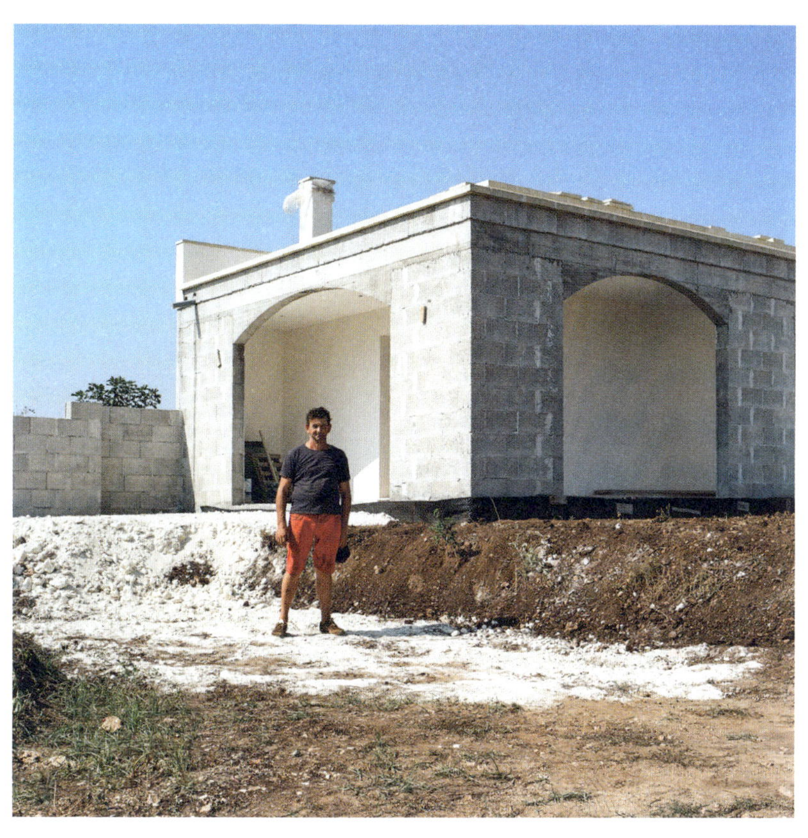

MINERVINO DI LECCE

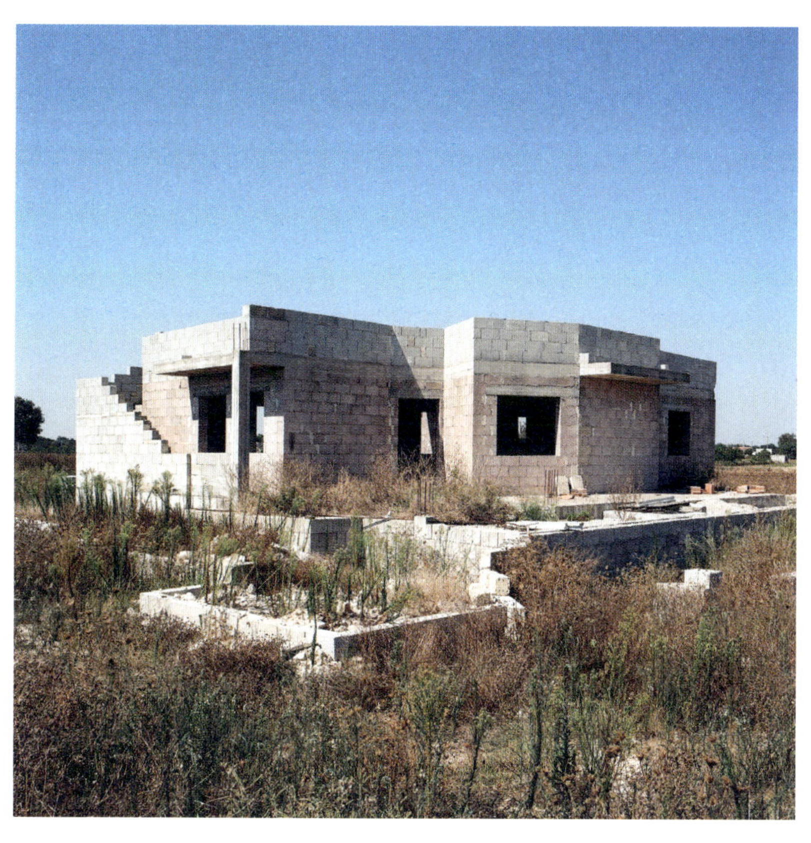

GIUGGIANELLO

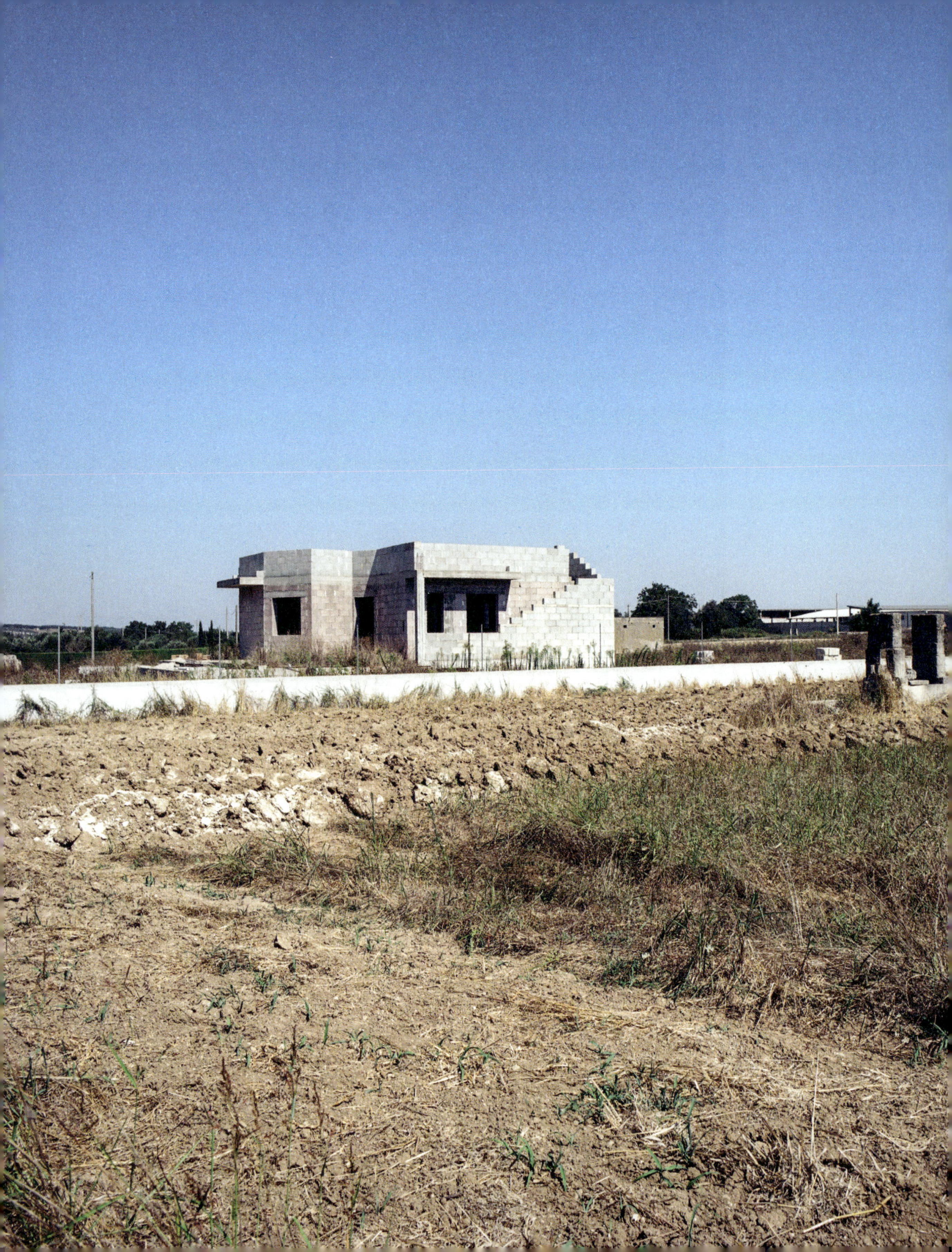

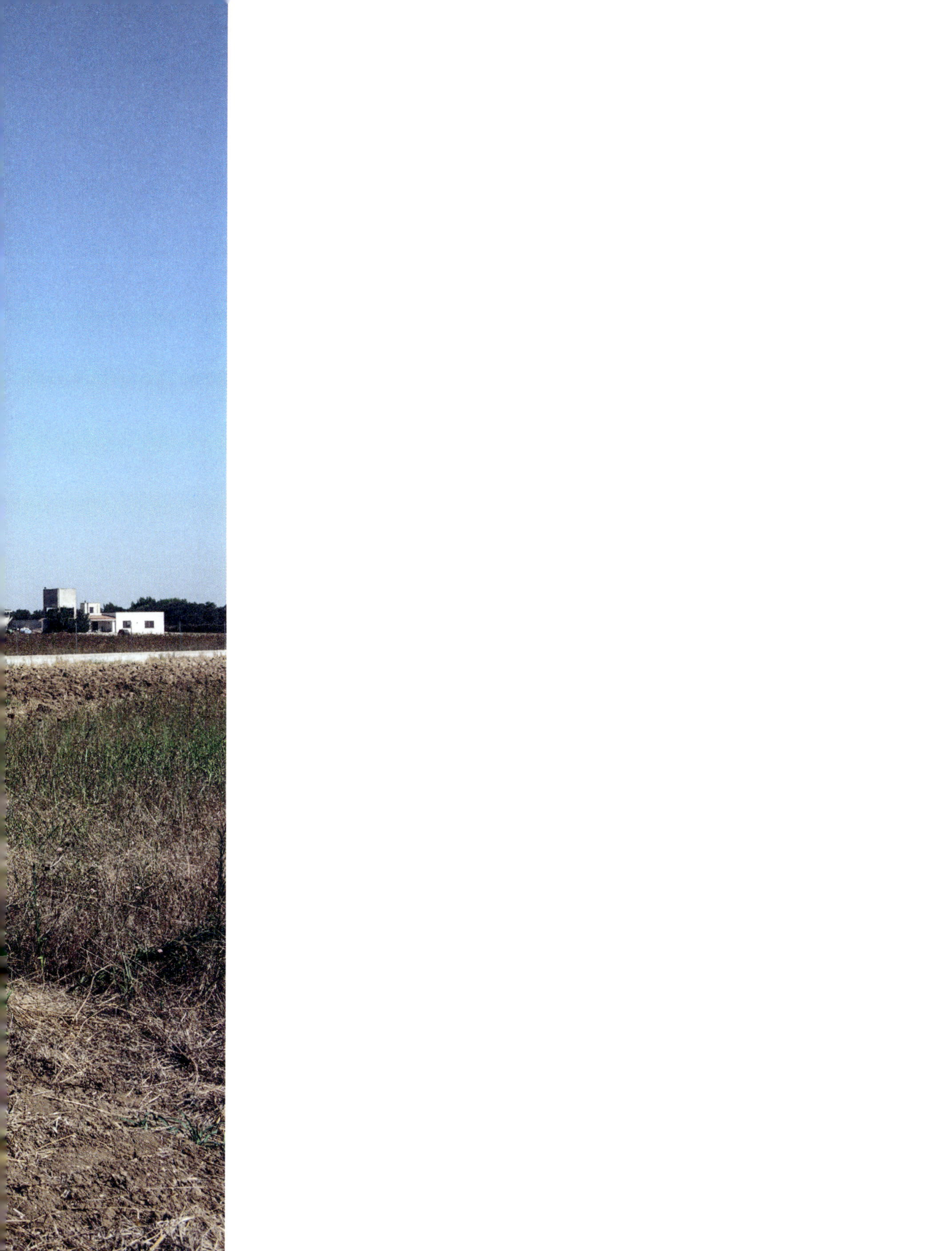

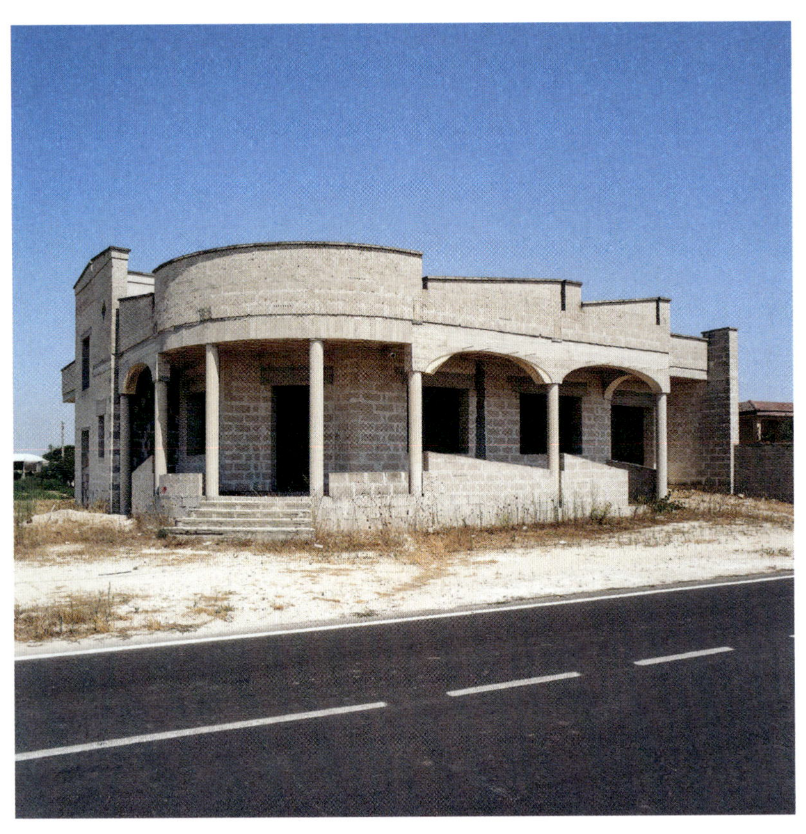

CASAMASELLA

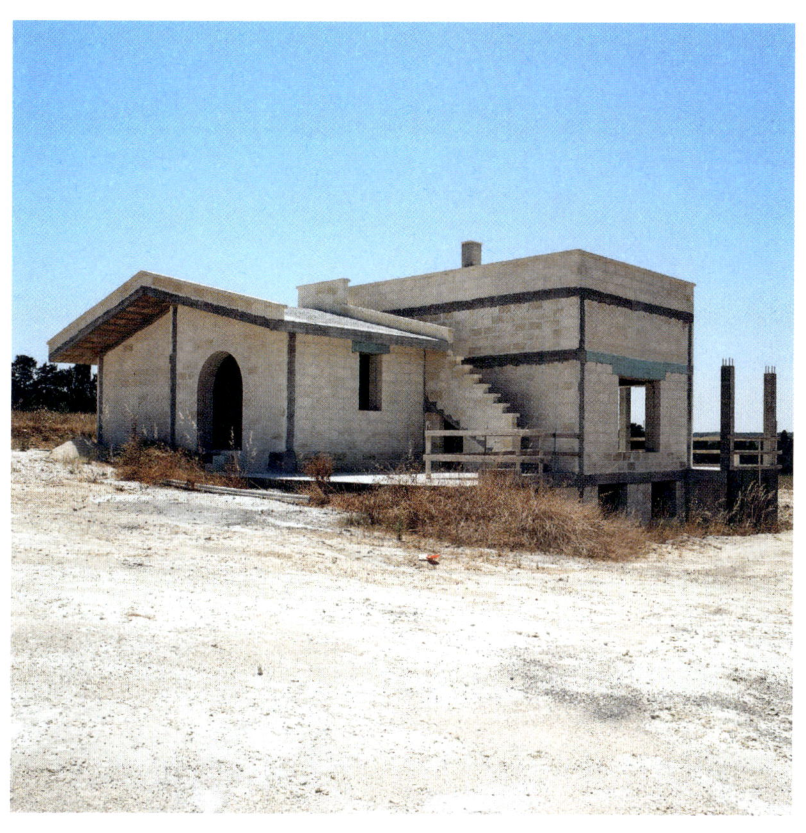

ALIMINI

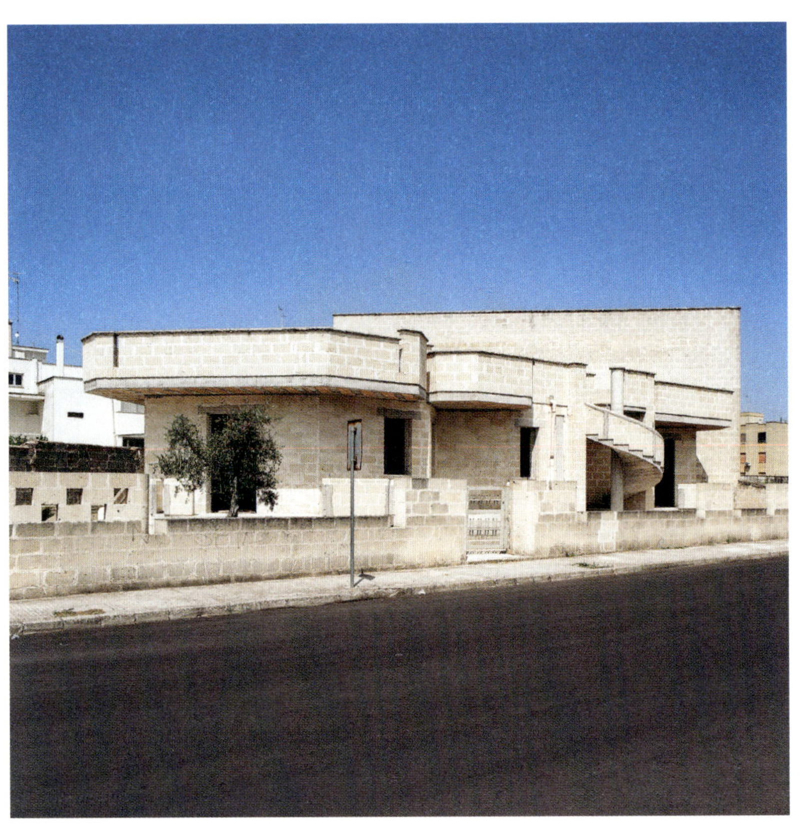

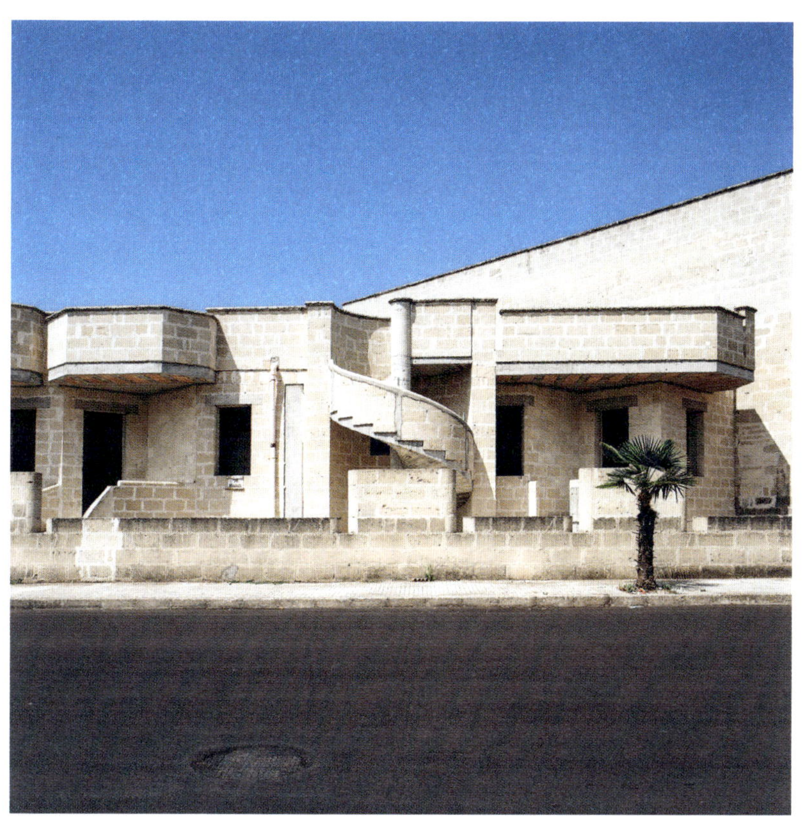

MARTANO

PASQUALE

A wall defines the boundaries of a house under construction, and yards and yards of gray cement occupy uncontaminated spaces. I have never liked the colour gray, but you can see it often where I live. It is the gray of houses under construction that will never be completed! It may be odd to say this, but I think that it detracts from our appreciation of the landscape, especially in a place like Salento, where the sea is truly splendid.

Un muro di cinta delimita una casa in costruzione, metri e metri di cemento grigio occupano spazi incontaminati! Non mi è mai piaciuto il grigio ma questo colore lo vedo spesso dove vivo: sono le case in costruzione mai terminate! Sembra strano dirlo, ma credo che tutto ciò rendi poco apprezzabile il paesaggio, soprattutto in un luogo come il Salento, dove il mare è davvero splendido.

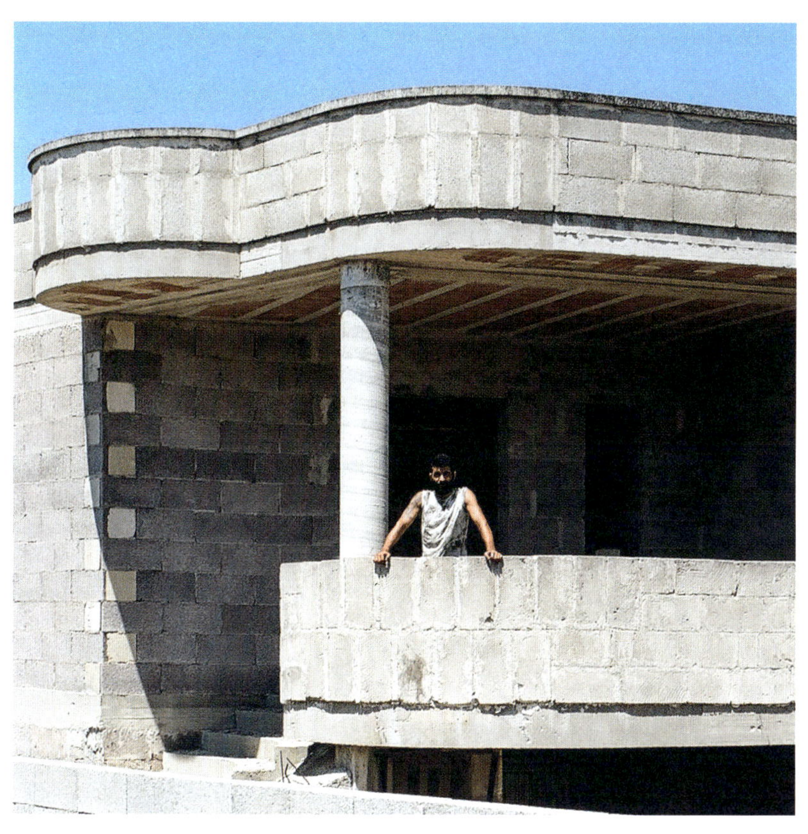

MINERVINO DI LECCE

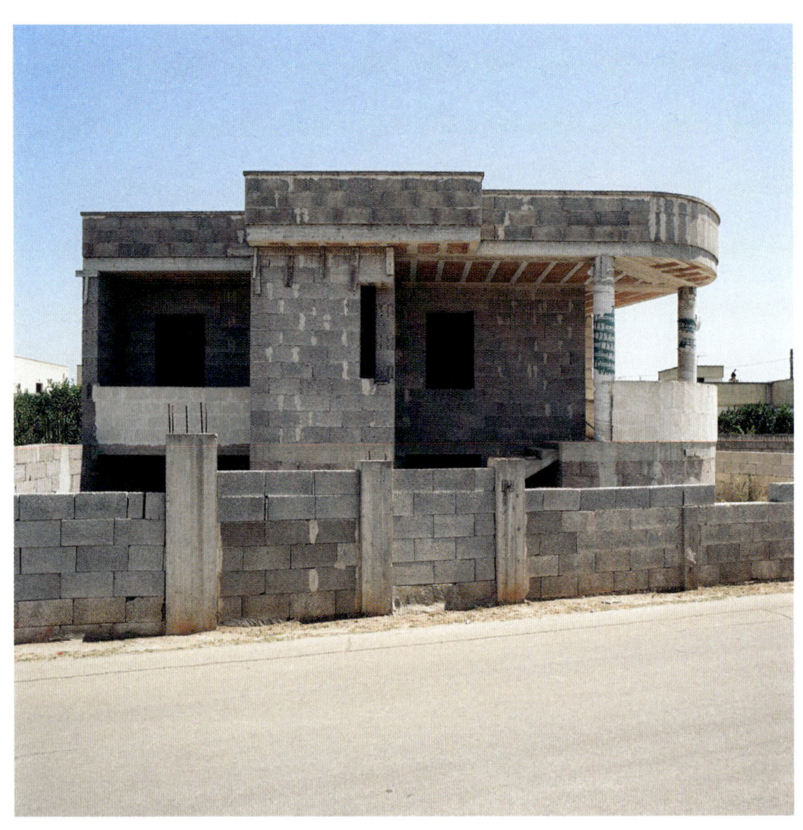

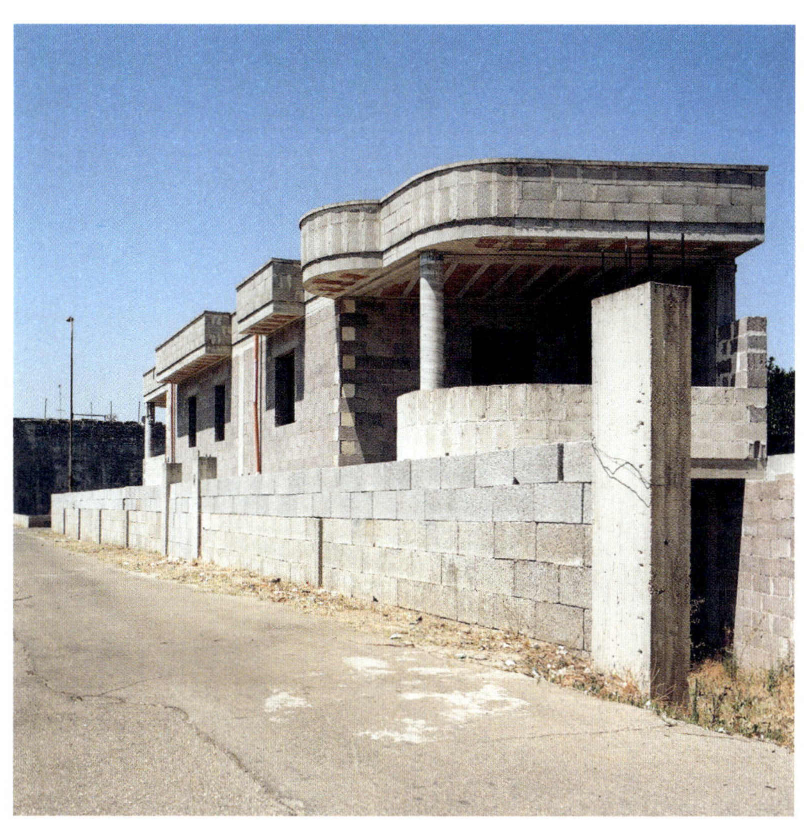

MINERVINO DI LECCE

DAVIDE

I have very strong ties to my land and all that belongs to it. We, the people of Salento who live far from our land, have "saudade" in our blood and this makes us proud of who we are. For me, it is a saudade for the red earth of the countryside, the sun, the smells, the sea, the lifestyle, the dialect, the food, the smell of the laundry hung out under the sun to dry, the taste of the *pane di grano* (wheat bread), and the dusty streets. As for these houses abandoned in the countryside… for years, our grandparents lived, worked and ultimately rested in these houses constructed with tuff. These houses can tell us what they have seen and make us fall even deeper in love with our Salento. They were constructed with the fatigued arms of our grandparents, who managed to do great things with little money. They are made of tuff and splendid stone in which, every once in a while, you can find shells and begin to fantasize and dream of wonderful things. I love Salento. I love my land. I love my roots.

Io ho un legame molto forte con la mia terra e con tutto quello che le appartiene. Noi, salentini che viviamo fuori dalla nostra terra, abbiamo nel sangue la «saudade» e questo ci rende orgogliosi di ciò che siamo. Per me è una «saudade» della terra rossa delle campagne, del sole, degli odori, del mare, dello stile di vita, del dialetto, del cibo, del profumo dei panni messi al sole ad asciugare, del sapore del pane di grano, delle strade impolverate. Le case abbandonate nelle campagne…queste case costruite con il tufo, dove per anni i nostri nonni hanno vissuto, lavorato e si sono riposati. Case che se potessero raccontare ciò che hanno visto, ci farebbero innamorare ancora di più del nostro Salento. Case costruite con la forza della fatica delle braccia dei nostri nonni che con pochi soldi sono riusciti a fare cose importanti. Case fatte di tufo, una pietra stupenda dove ogni tanto si possono trovare delle conchiglie e dove la tua fantasia incomincia a farti sognare cose meravigliose. Io amo il Salento, io amo la mia terra, io amo le mie radici.

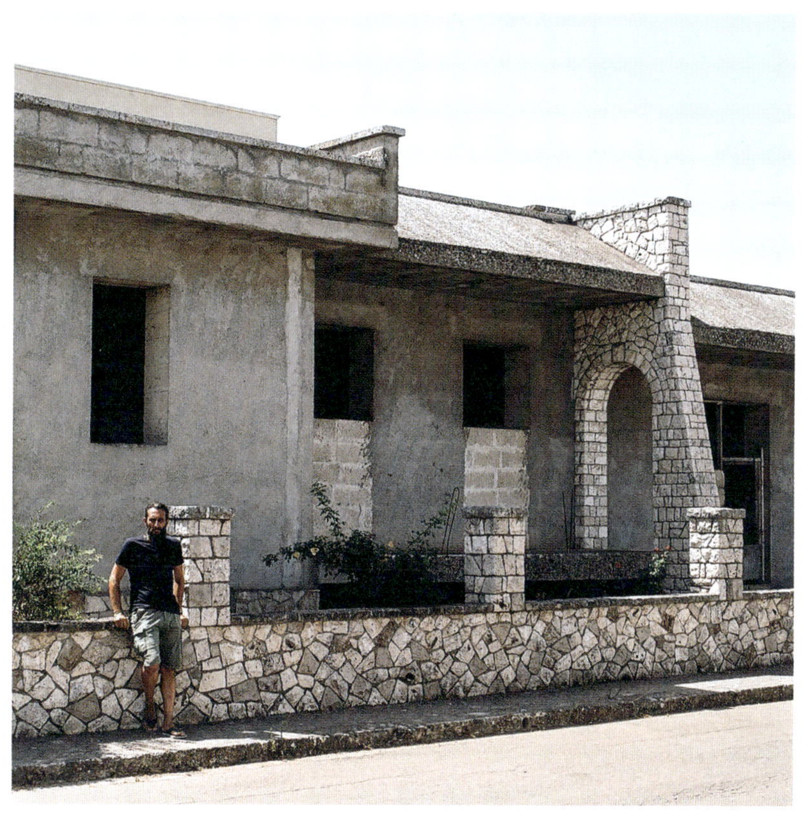

UGGIANO LA CHIESA

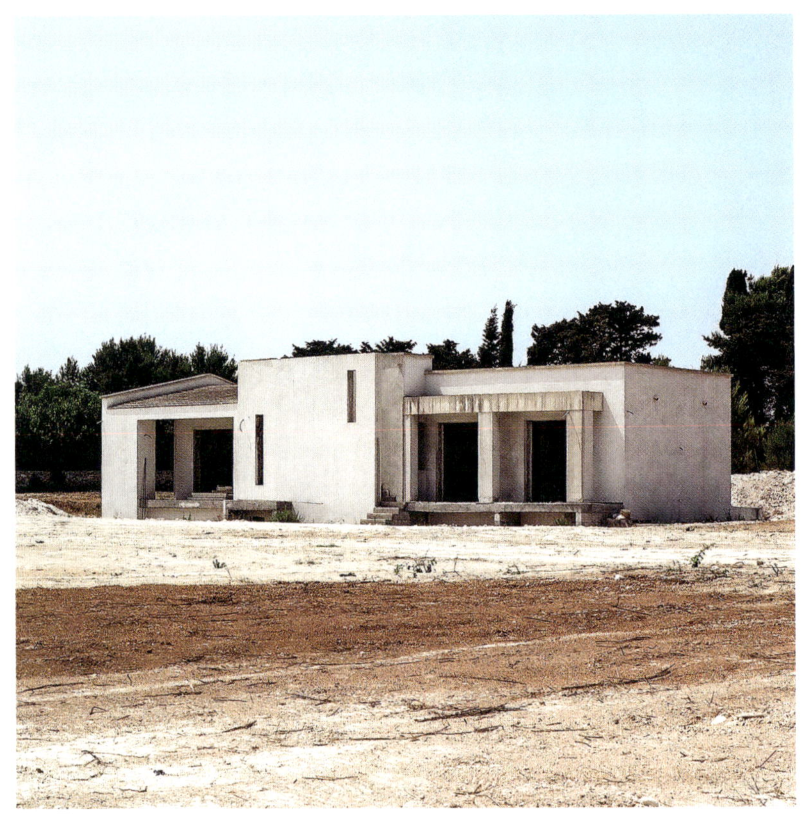

ALIMINI

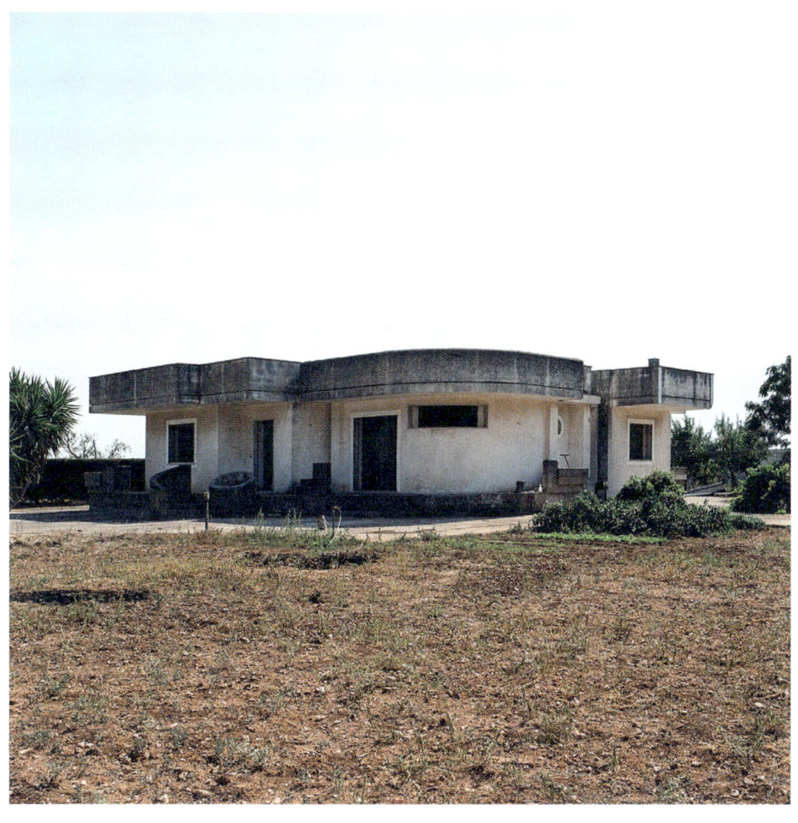

MURO LECCESE

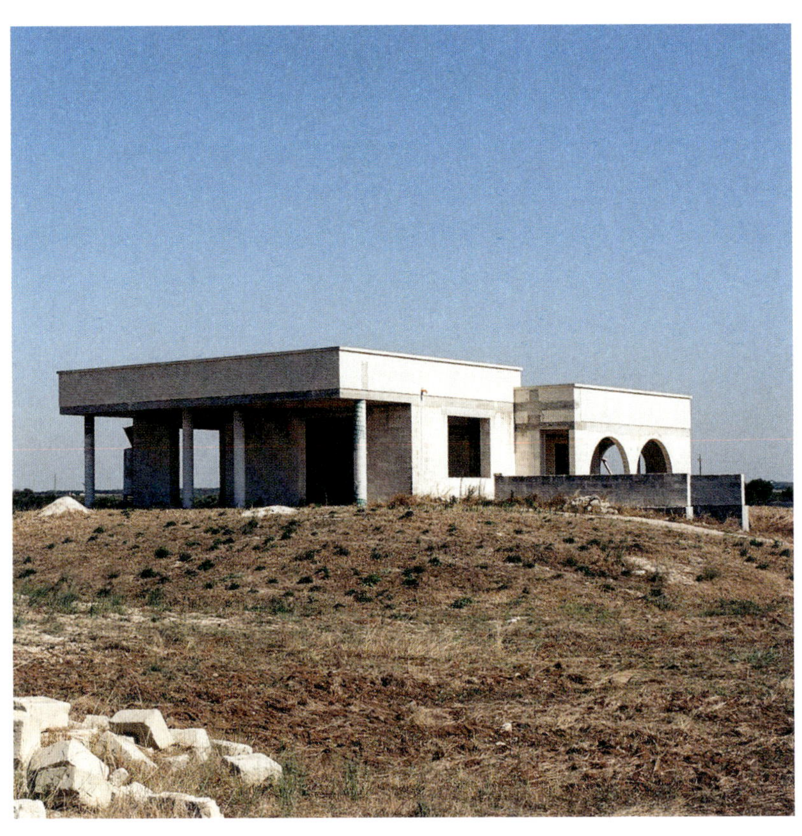

PALMARIGGI

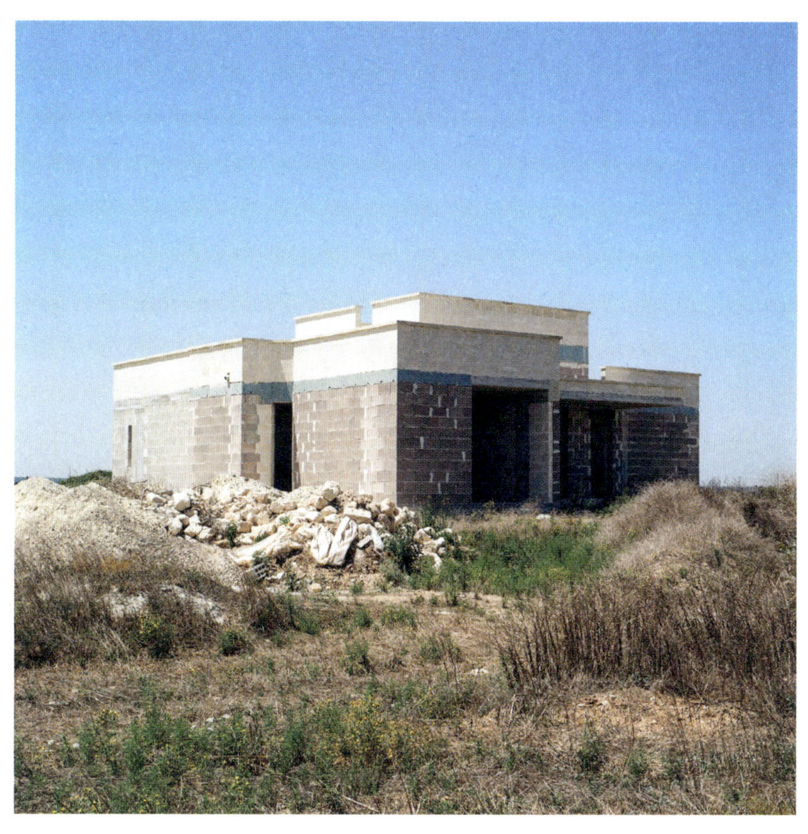

OTRANTO

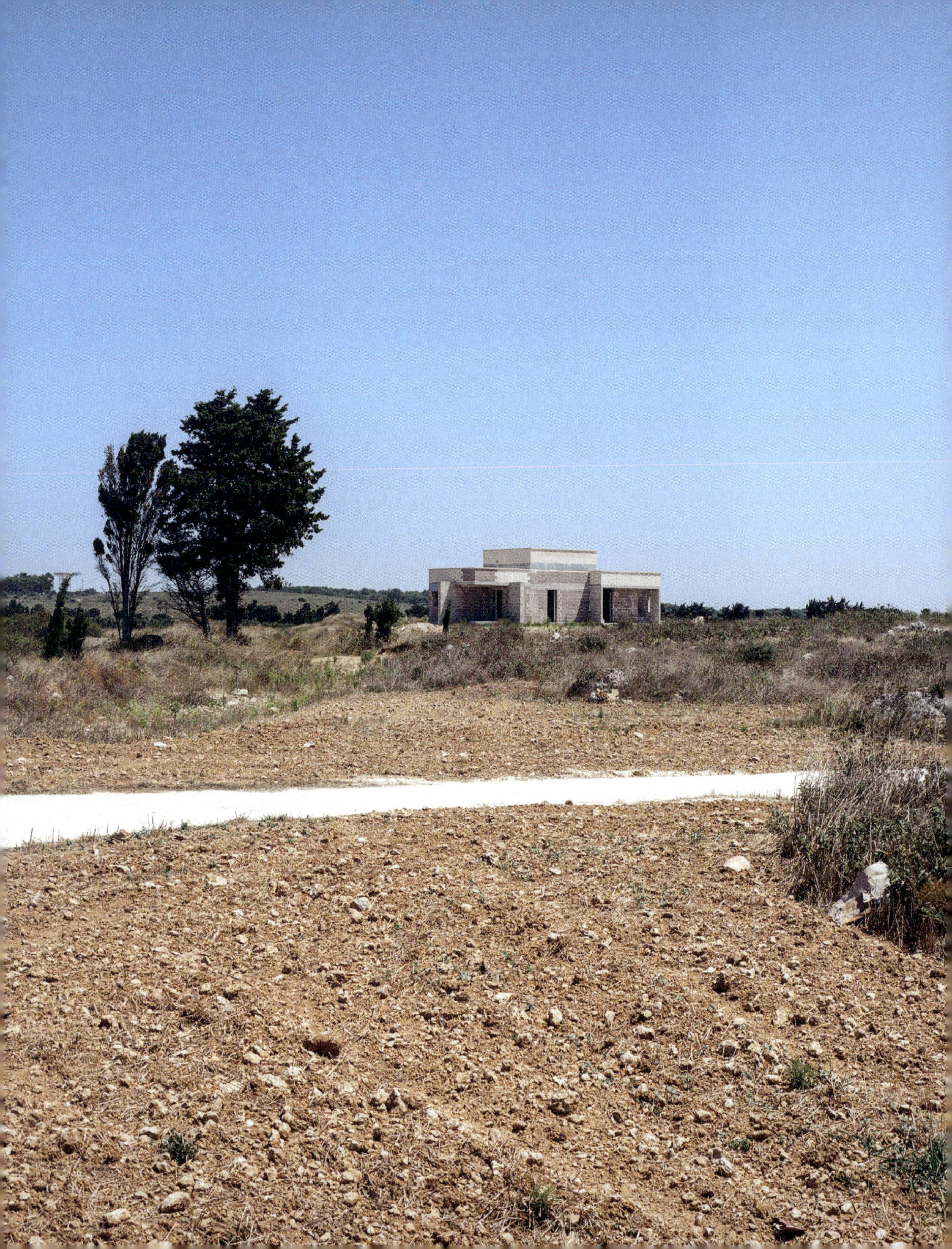

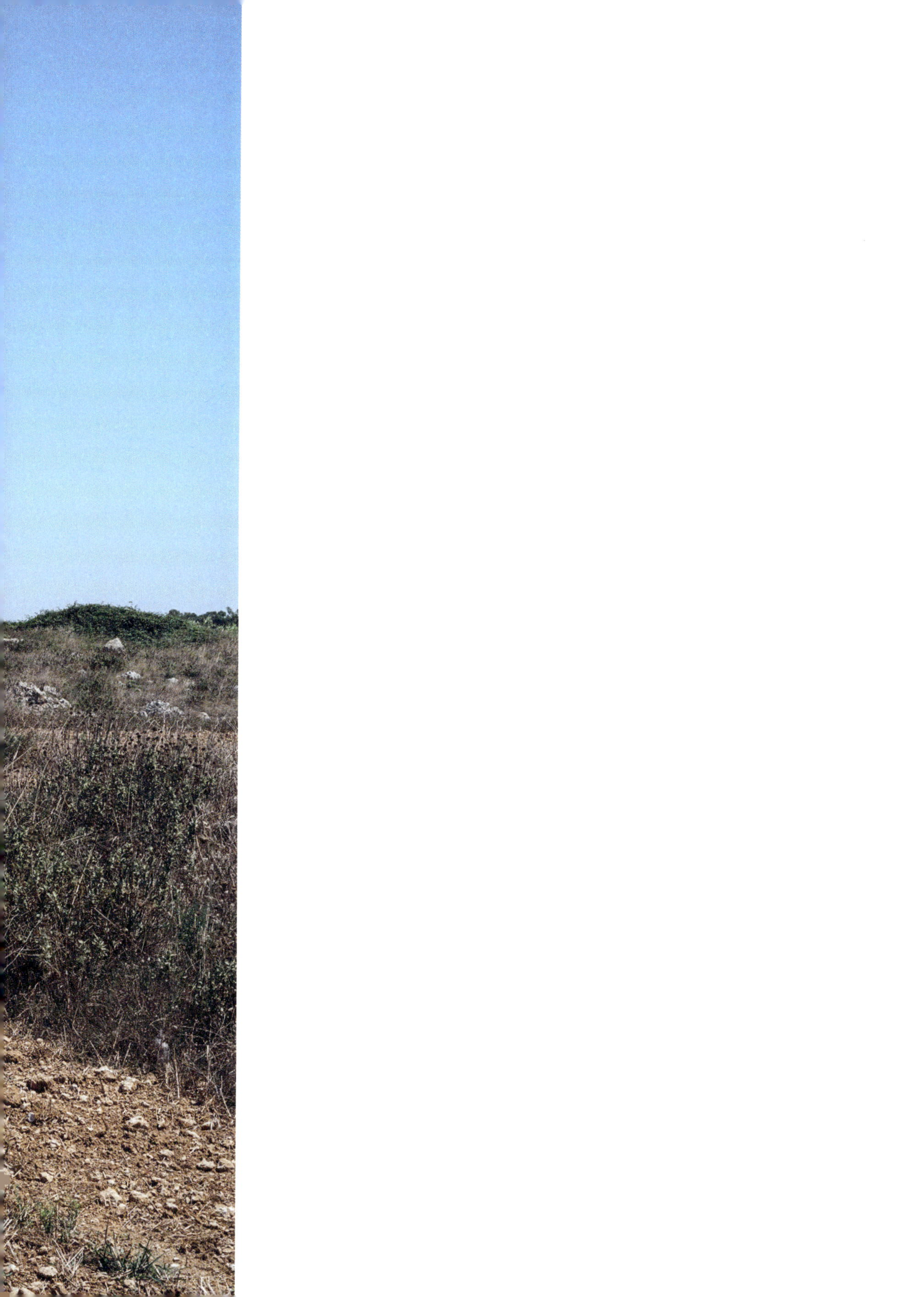

MARISA

Looking at these houses brings back memories of tuff, because when my husband was alive, that was his work. He was a mason! He constructed beautiful, strong houses. He appreciated the work that lay behind these houses – work that is hard and tiring, but full of fulfillment!

———————

Guardarle è un tufo nei ricordi, perchè quando mio marito era in vita faceva proprio quel lavoro, il muratore! Costruiva case bellissime e forti. Apprezzo il lavoro che c'è dietro queste case, un lavoro duro e faticoso ma pieno di soddisfazioni!

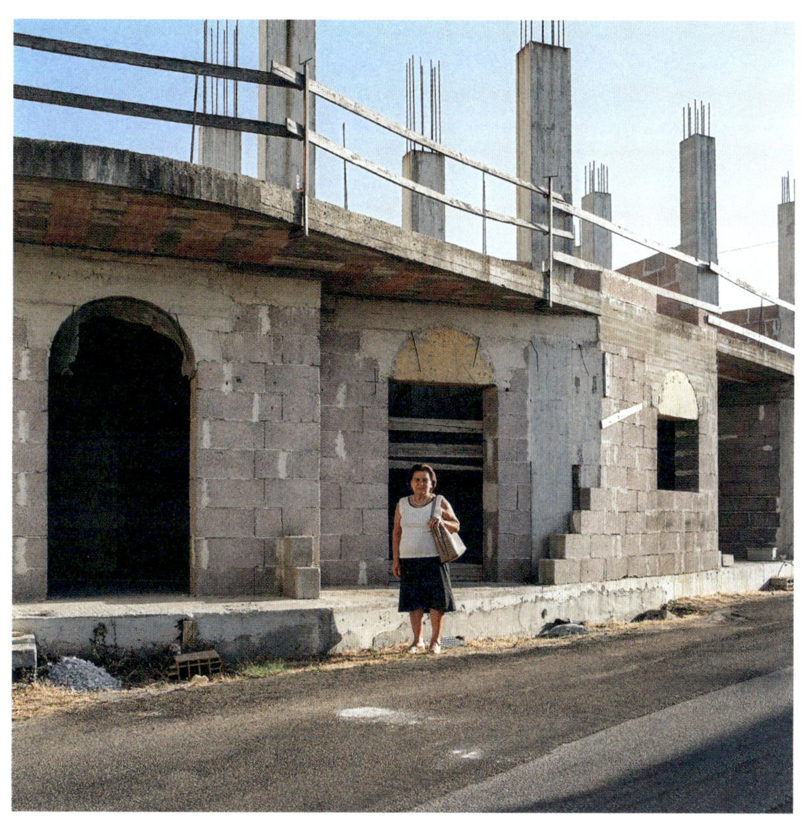

MINERVINO DI LECCE

THE ATROPHIED GAZE.

A HOUSE OF ONE'S OWN

Mariangela Turchiarulo
*Department of Civil Engineering Sciences and Urban Design,
Polytechnic University of Bari*

Located in the heel of Italy, the Salento peninsula once stood at the junction of communities and cultures. It was the land of the Messapians, a land of history and civilization that was once the Eastern star of Italy. It opened its arms to Greek refugees and was subject to grave threats from the Turks. After the opening of the Suez Canal, it united Europe with the Orient once and for all, as the "Golden Basin" of the Mediterranean.

This edge of Italy's Mezzogiorno, with its Middle Eastern traits and precious cultural, scenic and environmental heritage – the latter of which is gravely threatened today by the rise of the pathogenic Xyllela – maintains an alluring and dynamic local identity and now, more than ever, has a strategic role in the network of the Trans-European Corridors.

In this land of olive oil, wine and Baroque architecture, the Salento garden features a landscape of dramatically scarred olive trees and ancient, "noble" stone. Cicadas break into song on hot summer nights. Vegetable gardens overlook the sea, attesting to a lost agricultural civilization, and ancestral rituals still linger. Houses with courtyards, *mignani* (balcony or terrace that dates back to Roman times and is placed above the main entrance of a building to allow its inhabitants to discreetly participate in street life) and *ortali* (open courtyard behind the house containing flowerbeds and a vegetable garden) stand under a dazzling midday sun.

This extraordinary but infirm agricultural landscape, with its karstic forms, is defined by large silvery green expanses punctuated with olive trees and cut through with ancient roads. It is a fertile land of red earth and garden that is at once rocky and uneven and must be regenerated. It is intersected by small dry stone walls and rows of vines, and studded with *pagghiare* (dry stone constructions used to store farming tools), towers, fortified farmhouses, villas, old manor houses and wells.

The urban and the rural commingle and are at times confounded in a polycentric city-territory that is surrounded by the sea, almost like an island. Strong living traditions coexist harmoniously – almost cosmically – with the countryside, embedded in the palimpsest of the landscape. The city thus becomes an integral part of nature and viceversa in a model of settlement that integrates the agricultural production system that was once the primary reason for laying down roots. Urban expansion and the arbitrary spread of construction has often compromised this relationship that was serenely born out of necessity, eliminating stretches of nature and welding together neighbouring townships and the *forma urbis* once intimately linked to the morphology of the territory with a jumble of artifice and nature.

Rural areas have become a part of the infinite webbing of the radiocentric urban layout. South of the Plain, a dense network of small communities can be found embedded in the calcium ridges of Salento's Serre hills, lined up like rosary beads along the roadside. An indistinct polycentricity characterizes the city/nature of Salento. The houses dispersed in this agricultural mosaic are often illegal, contaminating the landscape of the Bonifica coast through voluntary operations that disfigure its traditional identity by unjustifiably using land that once was cultivated.

Gabriel Mauron's photography collection examines the phenomenon of "unfinished houses that have been constructed with who knows what hopes, but too quickly become old and uninhabited, new and incomplete. The vestiges of an abandoned dream" (Augè). Through Mauron's lens, these houses that are born to be ruins take on a poetic value and become monuments that invite us to imagine, experiment and interpret.

For little Davide, they turn into playgrounds to explore and to hide. These places are troubling and deserted, their suspended rooms attesting to silence, light, shadow, solitude and fear.

Mauron's photographs act like a spotlight, raising questions and inciting us to reflect. It is incredible how one's gaze becomes "accustomed" to everyday domestic landscapes, rendering objects – or rather, artifacts – invisible and nonexistent from a cadastral point of view, despite their physical presence. It leads us to view a familiar and incomplete landscape as a stable and definitive fact, rather than a moment in a process or a form in development. It is as though these everyday scenes subsist in a paradoxical harmony that no longer distracts the eye or the mind, as a certain permanence takes up residence in these open construction sites. The ugly becomes routine, giving rise to a sort of peaceful coexistence, without anyone expressing outrage at the unfinished state of these buildings, which date back to the 1980s and detract from the landscape – an atrophied gaze that reveals a problem of perception, inviting us to undertake a critical re-education process that may open our eyes to new visual and existential perspectives.

Mauron's photography brings to light scenes of abandonment and landscapes that are impure and incongruent, wavering between beauty and unsightliness, between order and disorder. These landscapes are paradoxical, dissonant and "misguided". They are works of contrast that surrender the in-complete and the in-finite to a more secular understanding that is free of any aesthetic or moral judgment that may naturally lead us to justify their incongruity.

Examining the context allows us to make sense of this anomaly. The homes photographed by Mauron are illegal offspring. They have not always been conceived out of social need, but following an infringement, remain partially formed creatures that do not conform to norms. They are souls that are condemned but nonetheless spared from Purgatory. They emerge like the skeletons of winter trees, bare and withered. Sometimes they are "legitimized" to no avail, fully revealing the obscenity of ownership and self-representation, as well as the uncertainty of a future that the owners once believed could be both better and within reach. The construction of a second home represents the sacrifice of parents for children, as they seek to make a secure investment to protect their savings, leading to a "tradition" that overrides any fear of penalty, sanction, or the derision of onlookers. In this race to "set up home", managing the construction of one's own house is encouraged from a cultural point of view, even if regulations are scarce and exceptions do not marry well with the necessity of safeguarding the territory's natural and scenic heritage.

A survey on the technical and formal reasons for construction – the kind that should always be carried out when discussing architecture and places – provides an interesting starting point to help us, in the words of Vittorio Gregotti, "find Man in each of his artifacts, whether beautiful or ugly, leading us to concern ourselves with putting forward a new fragment of truth of the necessary possibility from the contradictions of the past".

In a period of fifty years or so, the residing families – presumably immobile for generations in both a geographical and cultural sense – who are bound to the land and property have constructed these fragile landscapes of abandonment that have been photographed by Mauron. The patriarchal structure of the family is reflected in the configuration of what has been erected and the typo-morphological models of living. These multi-family and single-family residences provide the room to grow and make new additions. We can recognize the Dom-Ino skeleton, which makes it possible to gradually make one addition after another, thanks to the flexibility of the framework.

Nevertheless, it is a model that has been betrayed, often abandoned while unfinished, as new generations become "itinerant" in order to fulfill their own dreams, disregarding their parents' wishes to cohabit – parents who are not only buyers, but also ad-lib contractors and designers of buildings that may almost be described as "brutalist", with moss growing upon cement. They are beautified – if we may use this word – by an extravagant repertoire of decorative forms that are brashly juxtaposed with one another. Their mission is facilitated by the simplicity and economy of a construction technique that chiefly makes use of reinforced concrete for the support structure, and brick or tuff for infill walls.

These houses are not reliable in their static state, as they have often been constructed using black-market labour and cheap material in order to economize, and are constructed upon land that is almost always unbuildable. Without the proper authorizations, they violate every landscape and environmental obligation. Each day, the headlines attest to the new crises they must face as a result, including earthquakes, alluvium and flooding.

These landscapes of abandonment, in which nature attempts to regain possession of its space with all its force, do not only recount the past, but are the open wounds of a history that is still ongoing. They oblige us to reflect on how to prevent future illegal constructions and how to deal with ones from the past.

We must remember that institutions only began to view urban construction as a system of norms established for the conservation of the territory, rather than its development and exploitation, in 1985, with the implementation of Law 47 (Norms related to the control of urban construction. Administrative and legal sanctions). It is only recently that the Piano Paesaggistico Territoriale della Regione Puglia (Puglia Regional Territorial Landscape Plan) has brought about a cultural revolution in Pugliese society, teaching us that the landscape is about *amor loci* – a love of one's place. In order to elevate both rural and urban areas, city and country must come to an agreement. By developing construction projects and respecting rules that safeguard the landscape and conceive of the production of the territory as a "common good", we can nurse the atrophied gaze and engender opportunities to evolve, without which, as Adolf Loos would say, "no dissonance can be instilled in this peace".

Bibliography

Augé, Marc, *Rovine e macerie. Il senso del tempo*, Turin, Bollati Boringhieri, 2004.

Destro, Nicola. *Geografia delle case deboli. Oltre l'abusivismo edilizio.* 2013. University of Padova, PhD dissertation.

Loos, Adolf. "Architektur." *Der Sturm,* 15 December 1910.

Licata, Gaetano. *Maifinito.* Macerata, Quodlibet Studio, 2014.

Magnaghi, Alberto. "La costruzione sociale del Piano: metodi, obiettivi, strategie. Il Piano Paesaggistico alla prova pubblica." *Quaderni del Paesaggio n. 3, Atti del Primo Ciclo delle Conferenze d'Area del PPTR,* Altamura, 10 December 2008; Acaya (Vernole) 12 December 2008; Lucera, 15 December 2008, pp. 7-29.

Masetto, Nicoletta. "Il respiro delle case abbandonate." *Messaggero di sant'Antonio,* 4 July 2016.

Montemurro, Michele. *Le terre. Borghi murati.* Florence, Aión Edizioni, 2018.

Palumbo, Pier Fausto. "Caratteri e aspetti di una civiltà salentina." *Studi salentini,* June 1956, pp. 3-10.

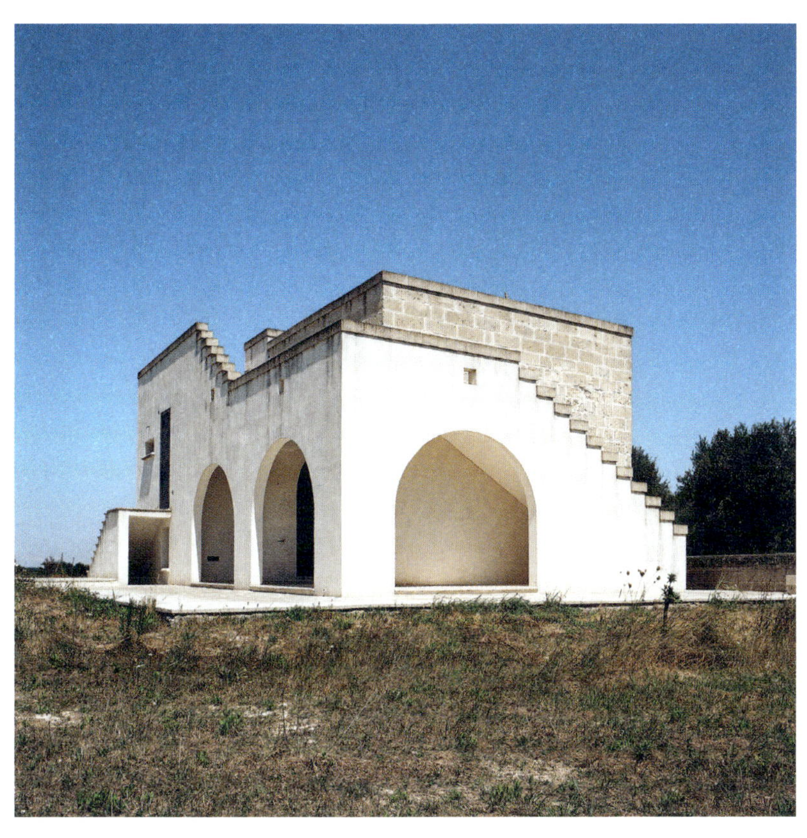

PORTO BADISCO

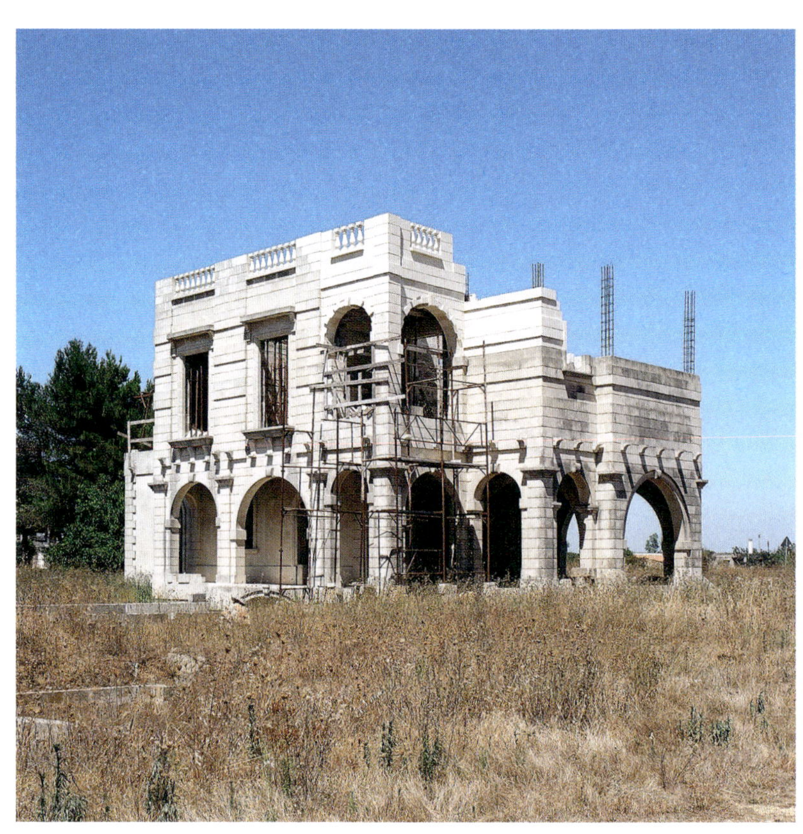

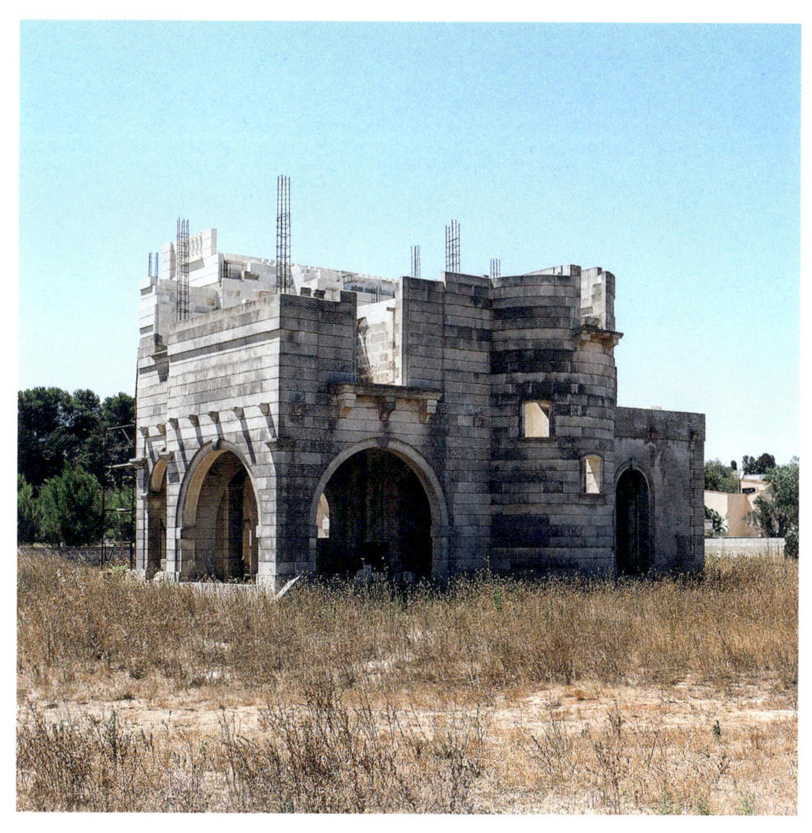

SCORRANO

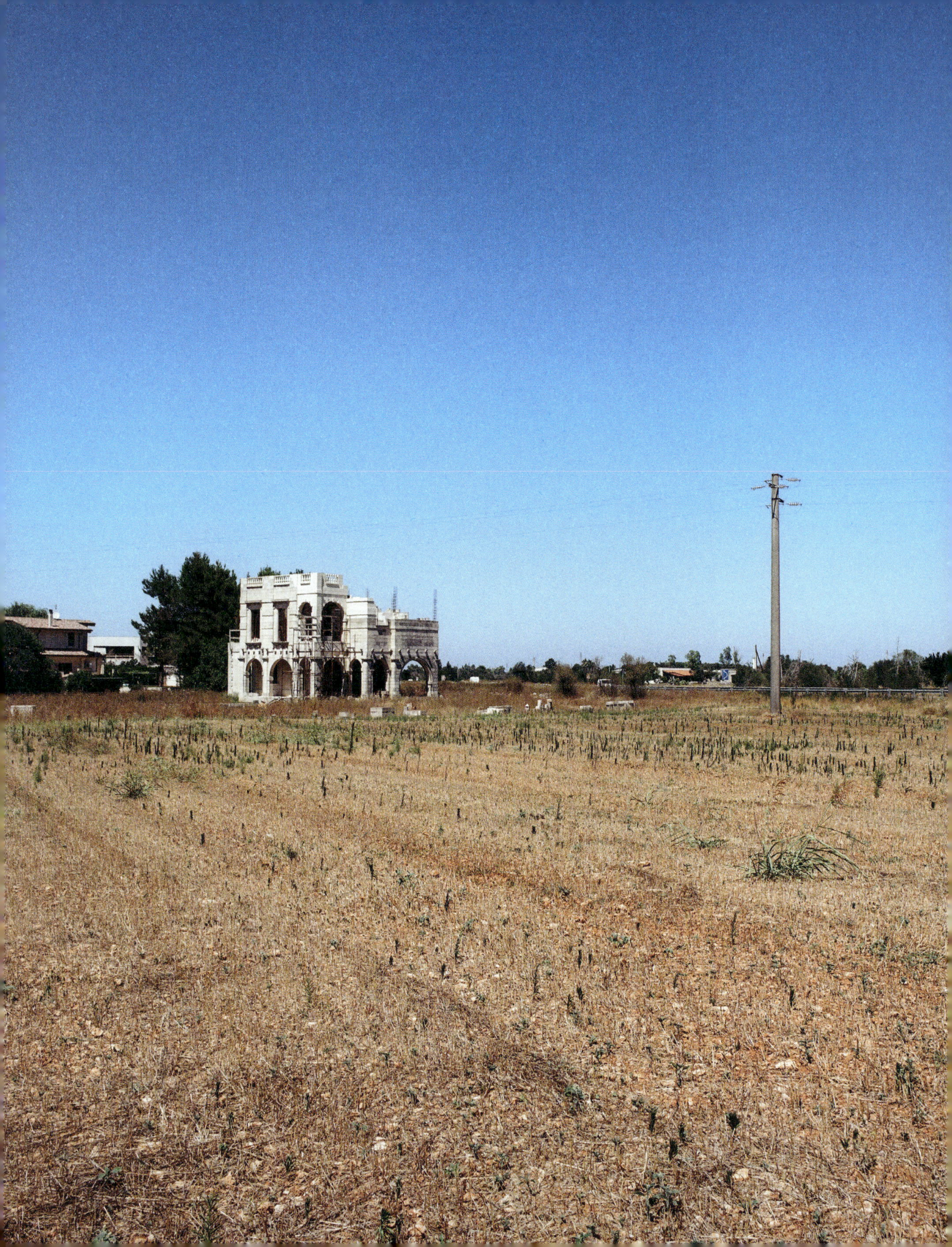

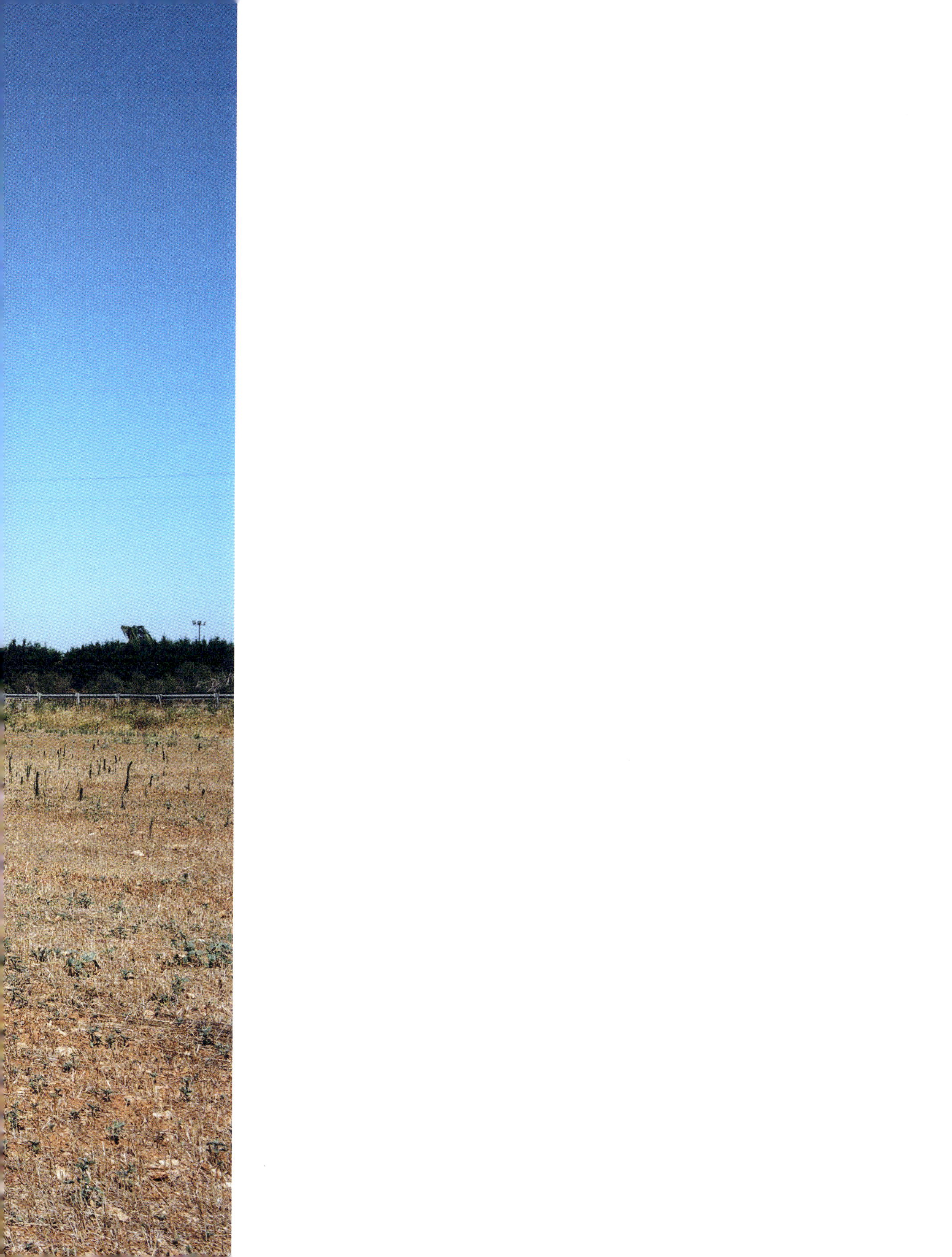

GEMMA AND ANTONIO

The panorama of Salento, all that countryside, is an added value for the house! A house that is open to a very appealing landscape!

———————

Il panorama salentino, tutto di campagna, dà un valore aggiunto alla casa! Una casa che si apre verso l'esterno in un paesaggio molto suggestivo!

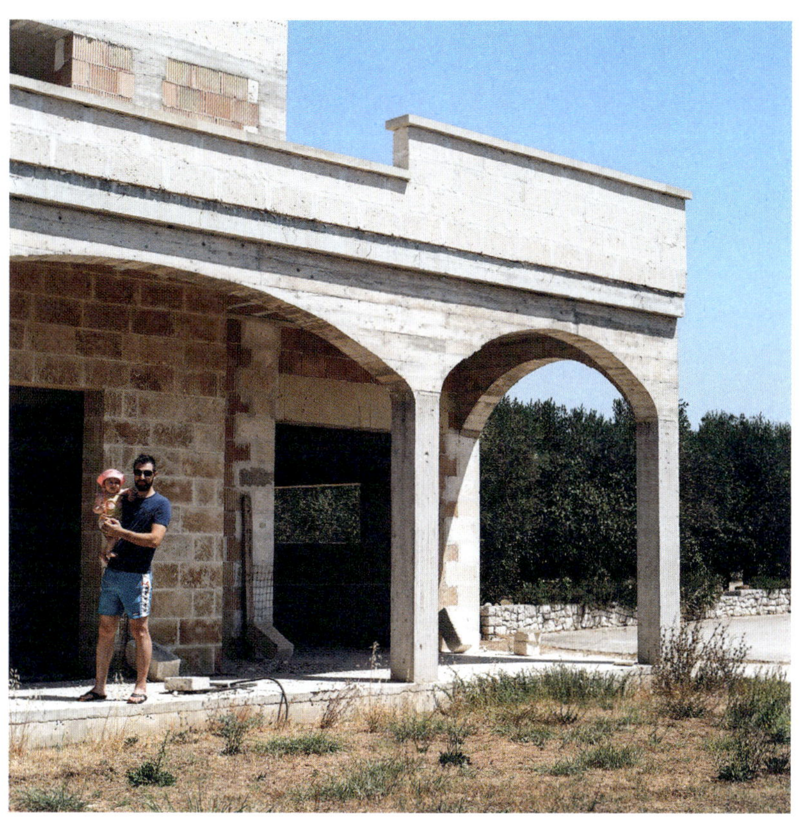

UGGIANO LA CHIESA

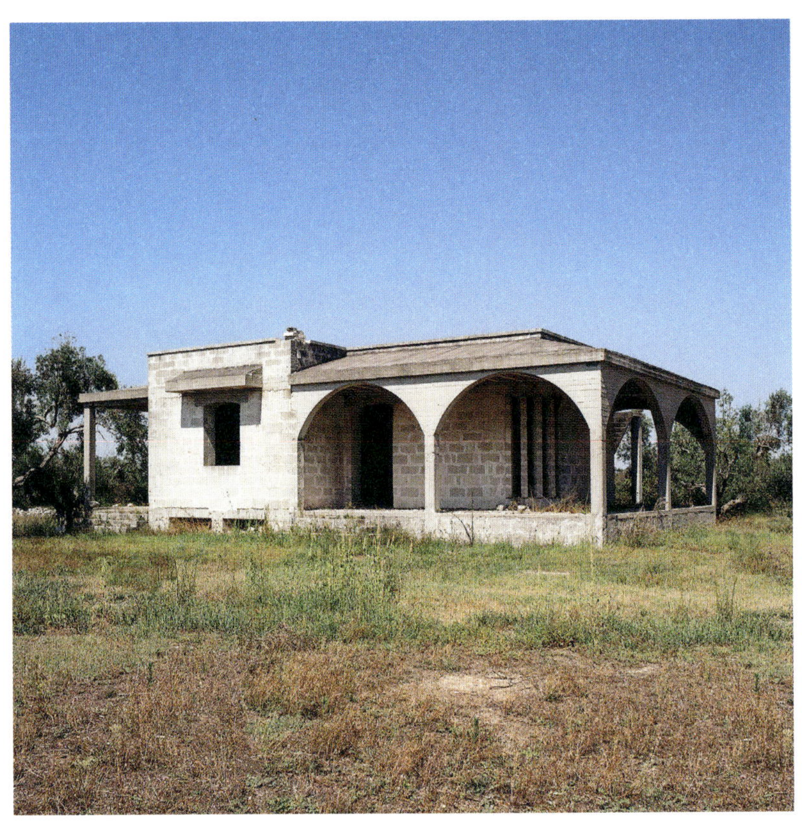

ZOLLINO

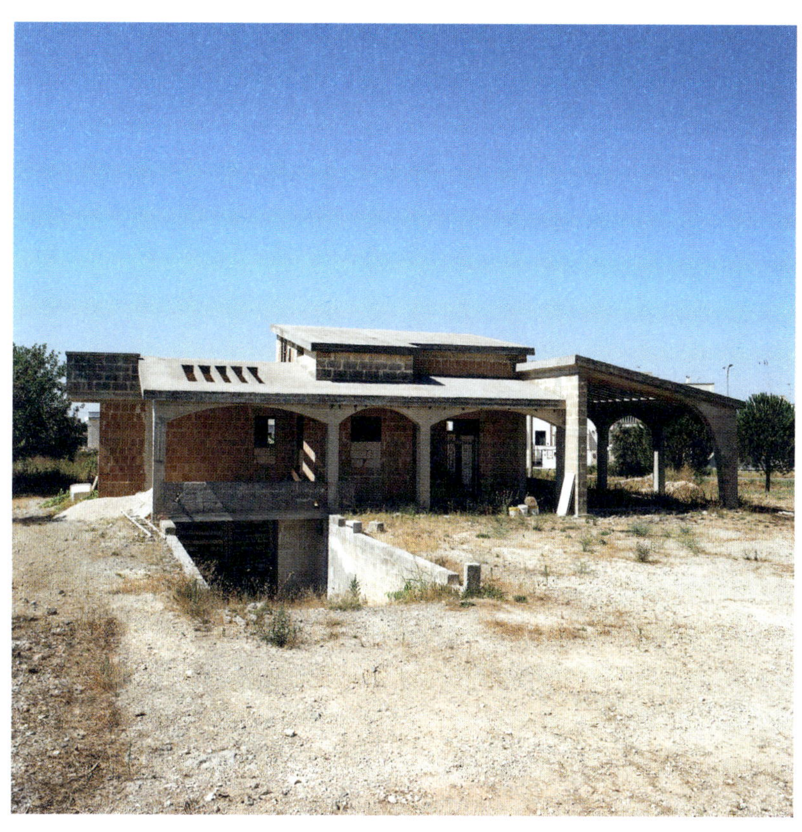

SPONGANO

LORENZO

We grew up with the desire to build our own house. We knew that we would have to make great sacrifices, but that they would surely be worth it.

Sin da piccoli cresciamo con la voglia di realizzare la nostra casa, consapevoli di dover affrontare enormi sacrifici ma che sicuramente ne valgono la pena.

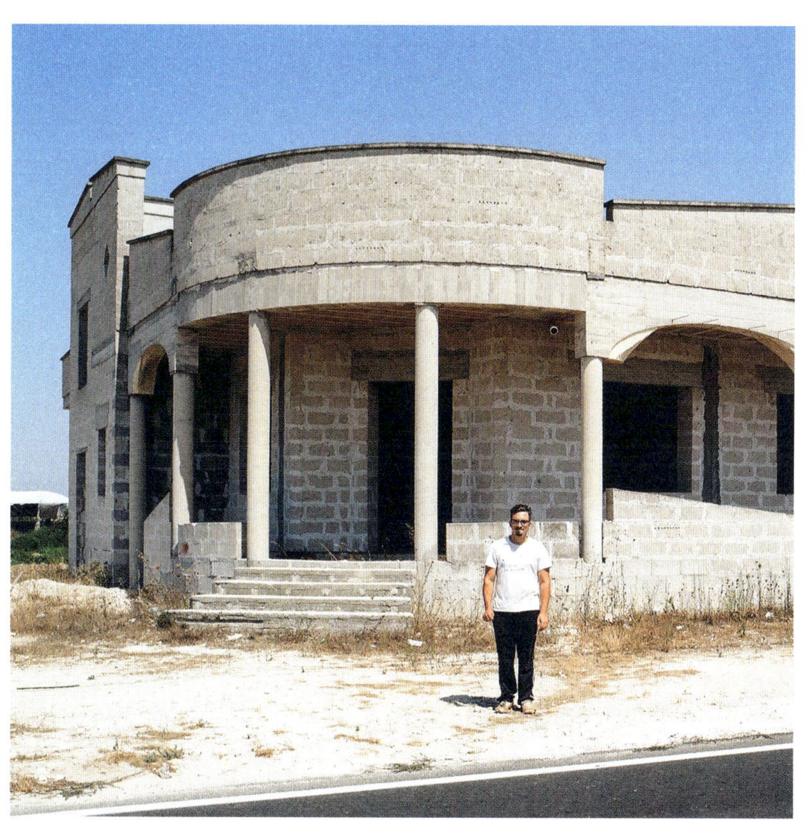

CASAMASSELLA

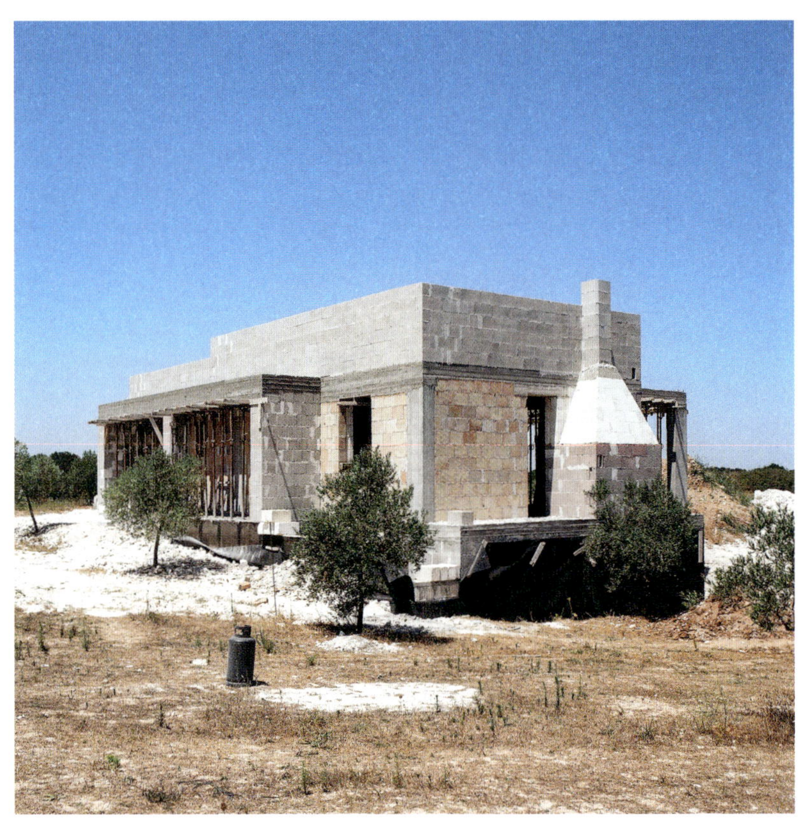

MOROMONTE

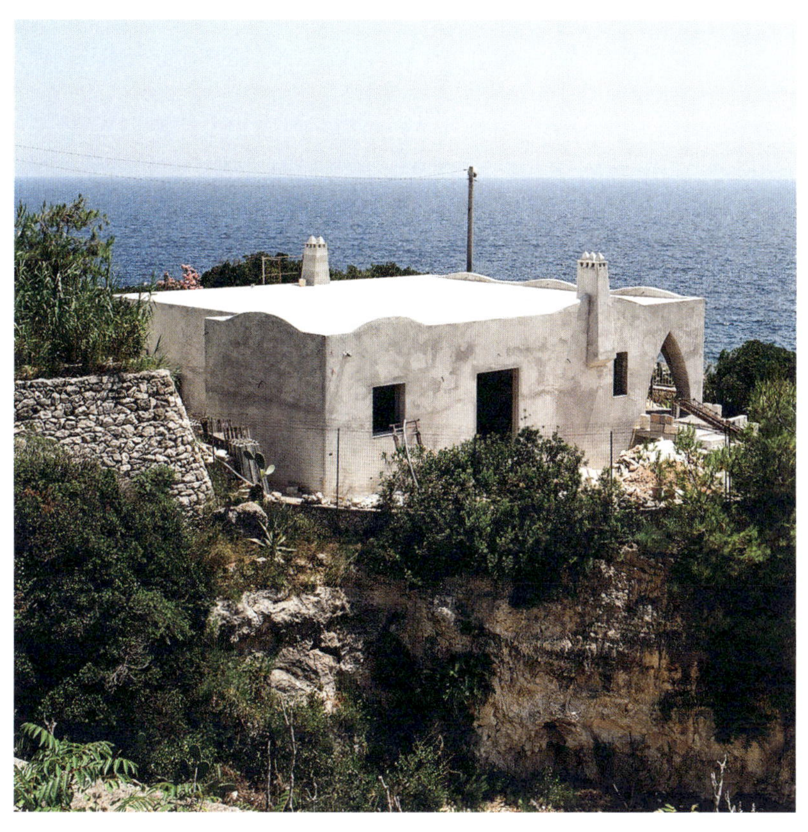

TRICASE PORTO

SILVIO

It is a shame to keep these houses in construction on hold. Maybe the banks should help out if people are unable to finish them.

———

Tenere ferme queste case in costruzione è un gran peccato. Forse le banche dovrebbero aiutare a finirle perchè magari la gente non ha la possibilità di portarle a termine.

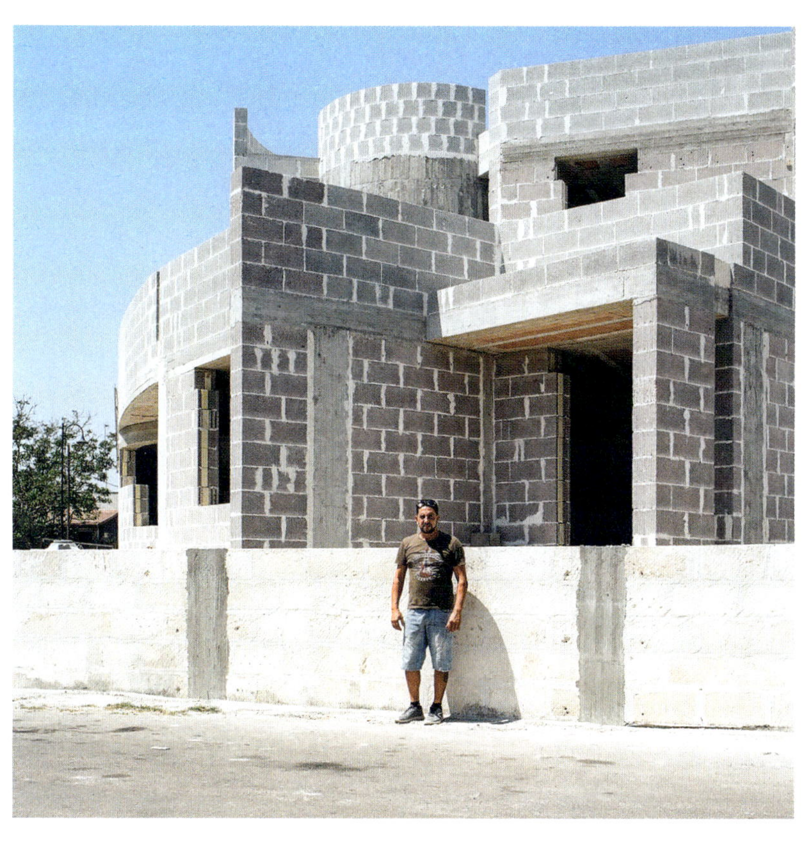

MINERVINO DI LECCE

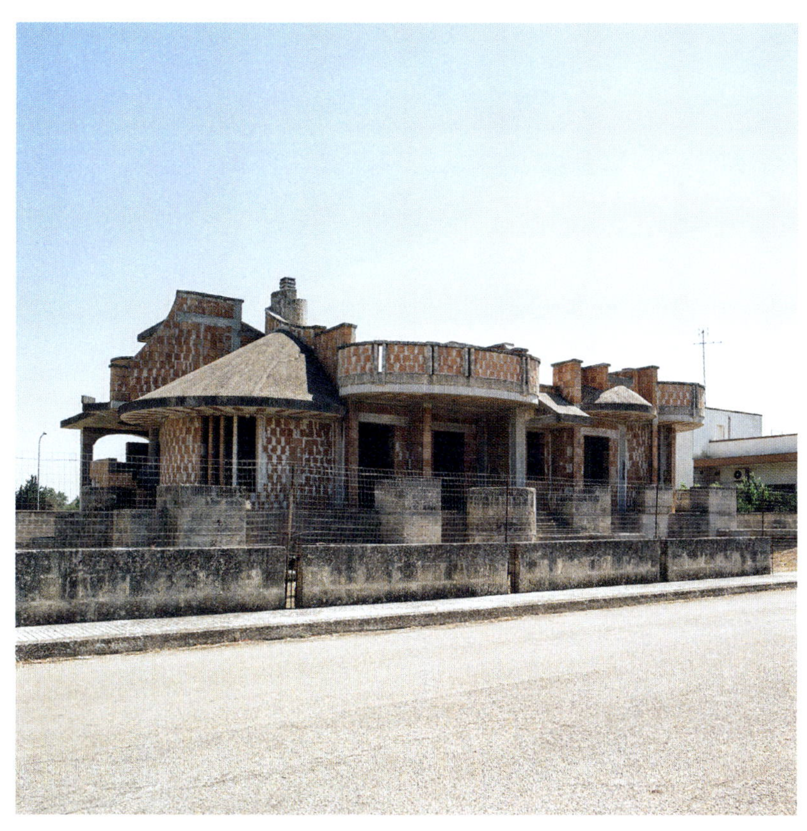

ZOLLINO

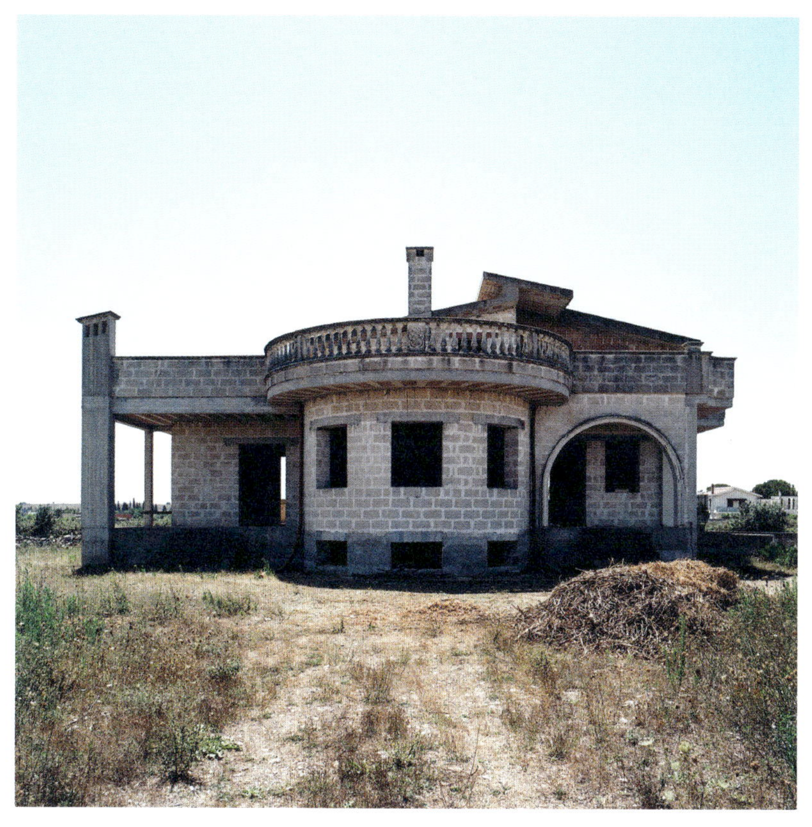

STERNATIA

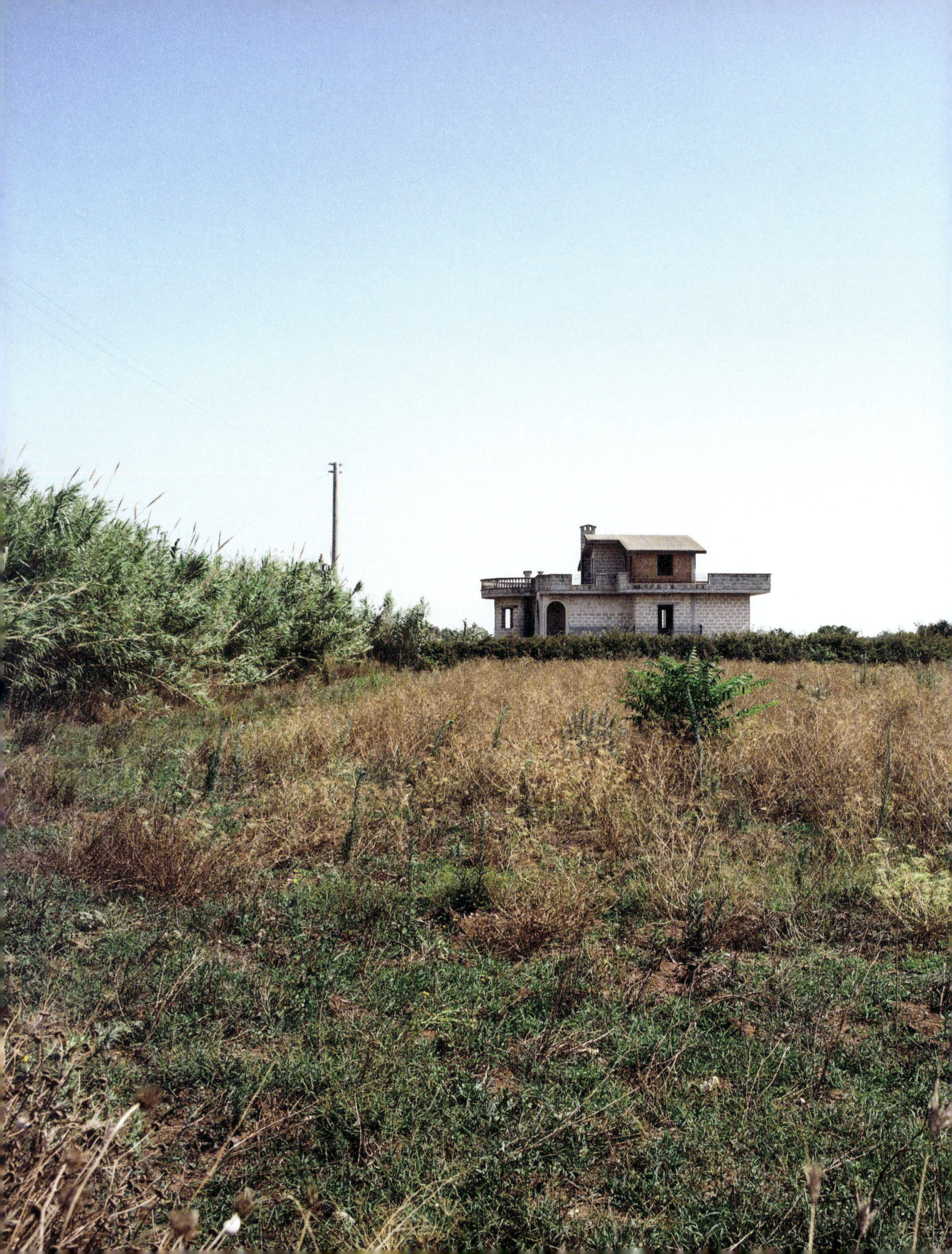

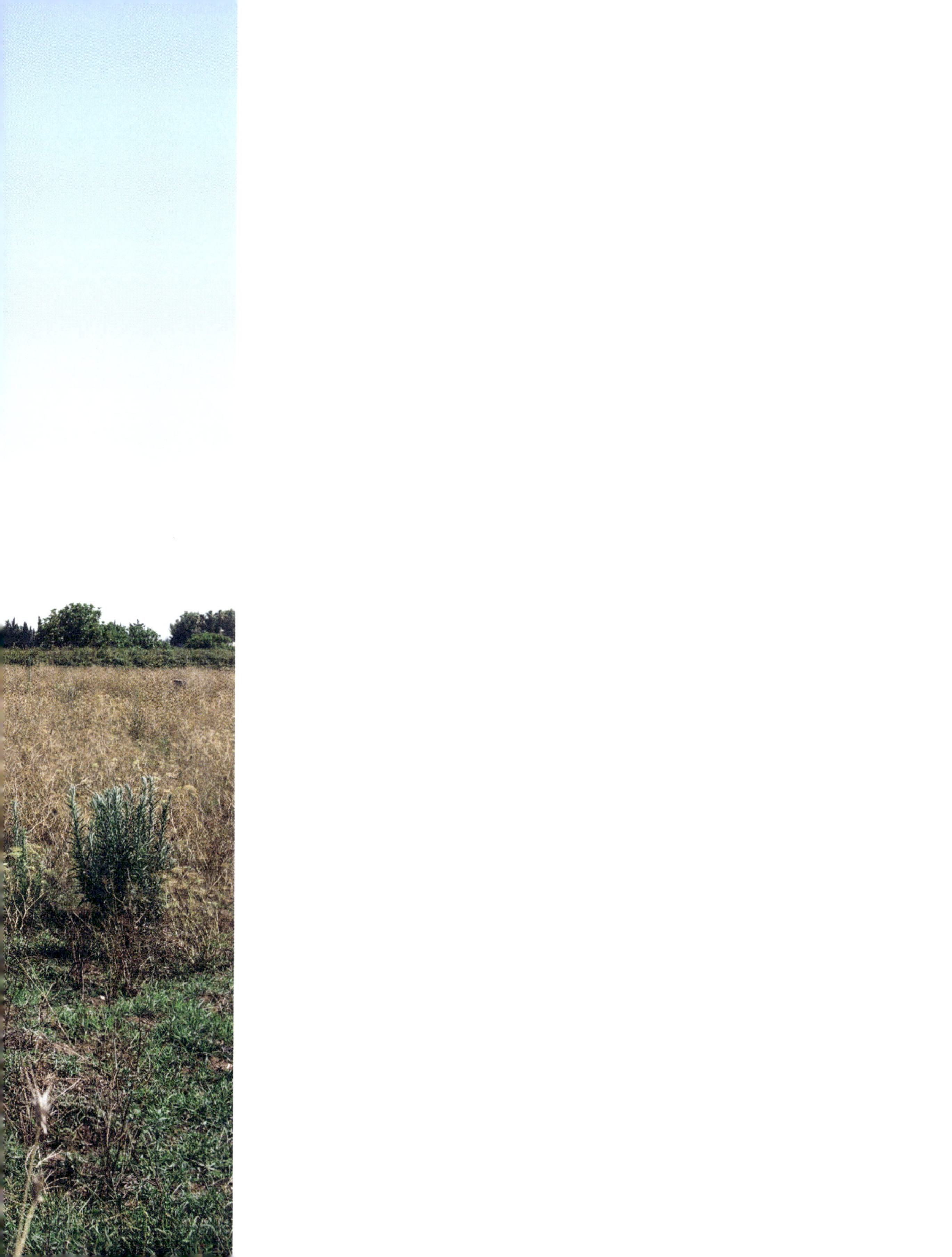

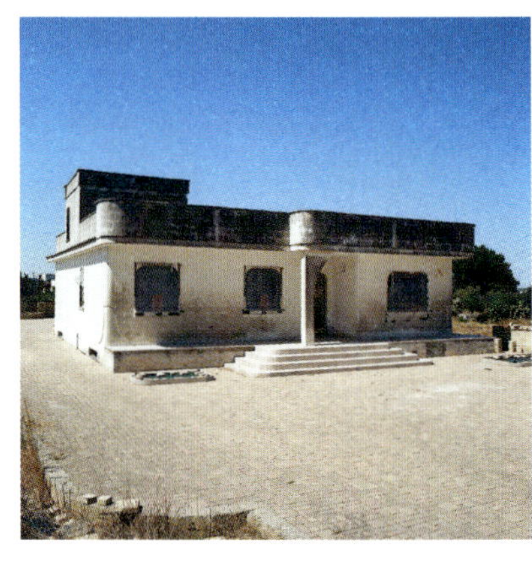
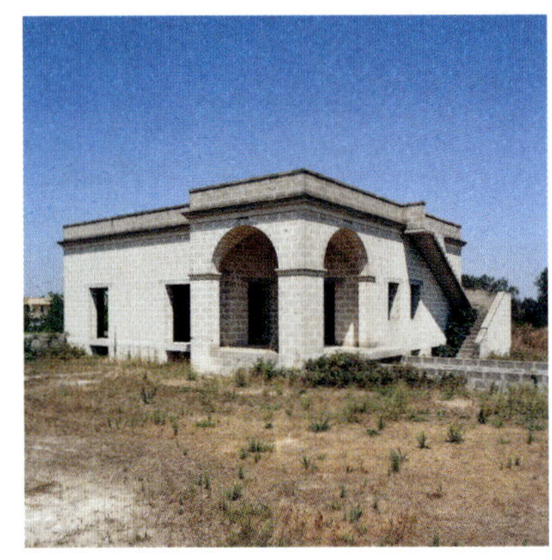
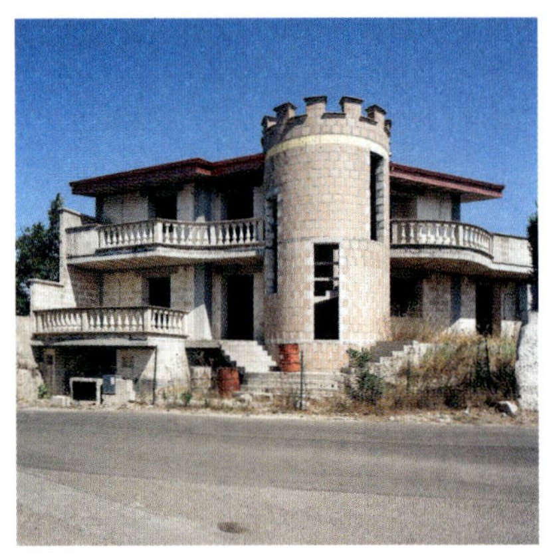
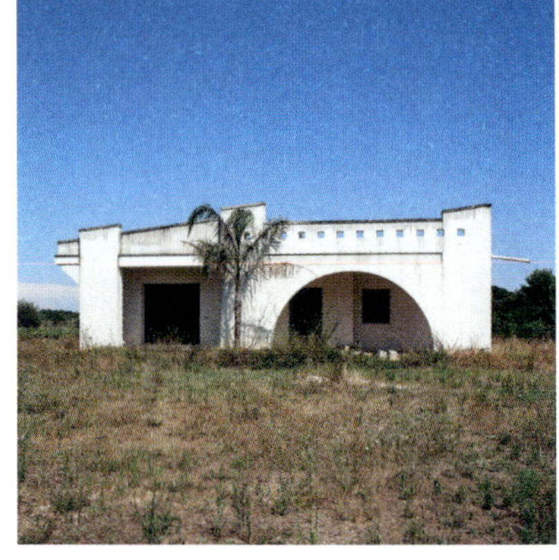
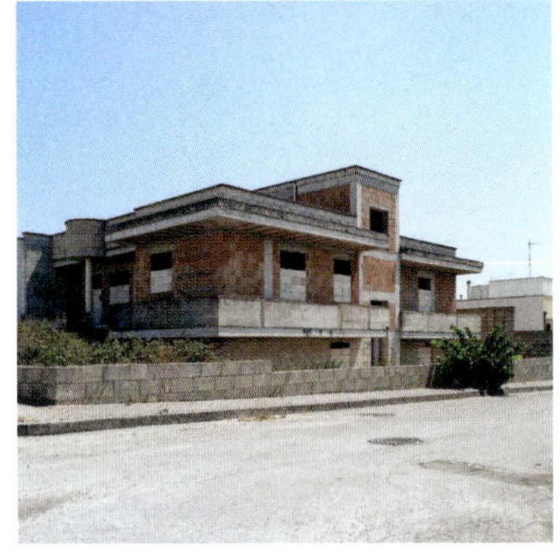
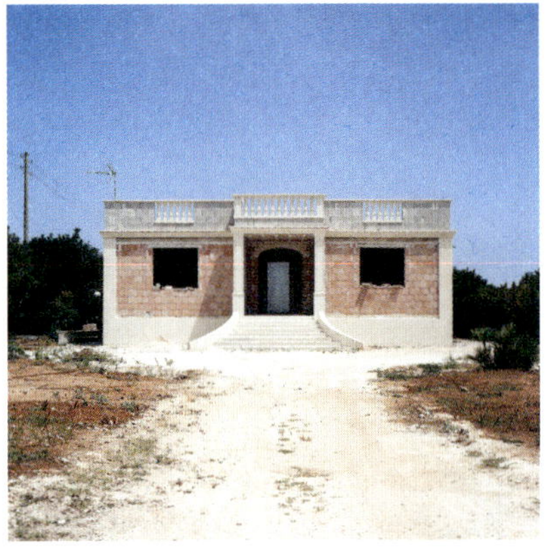
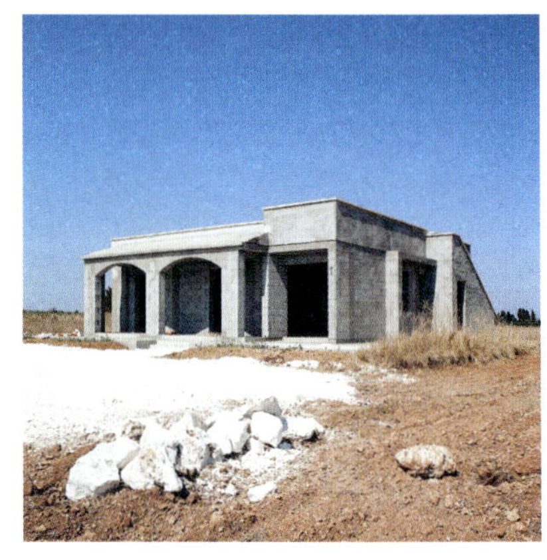
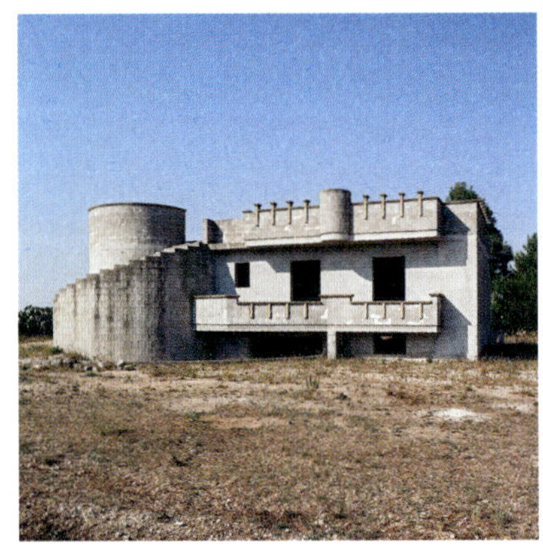
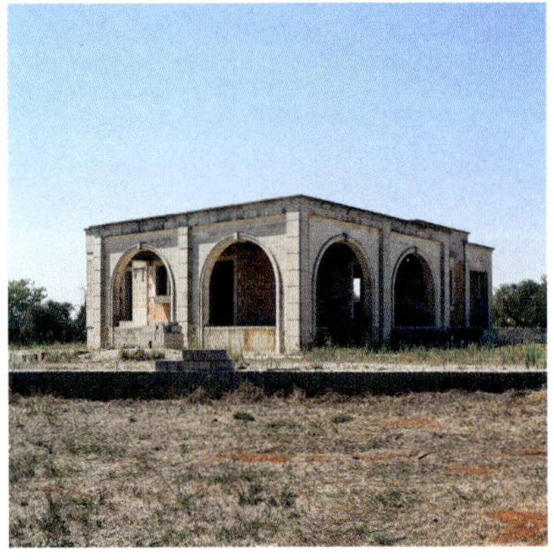
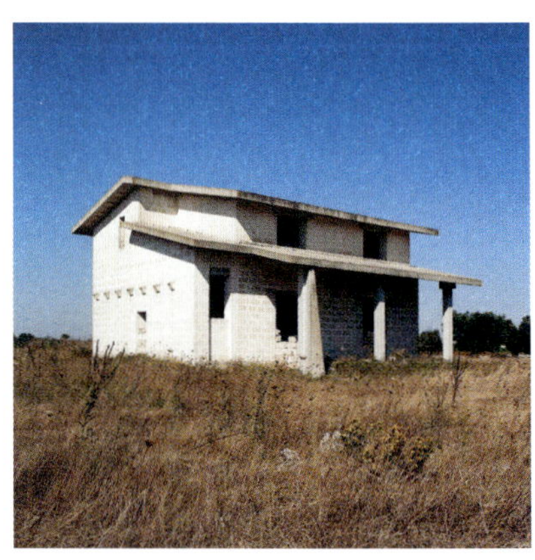
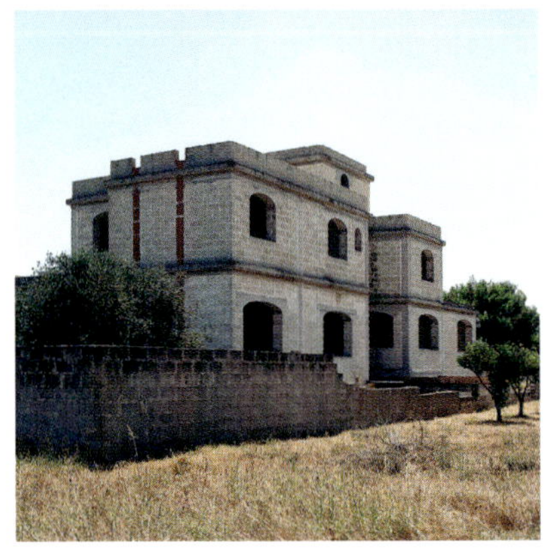
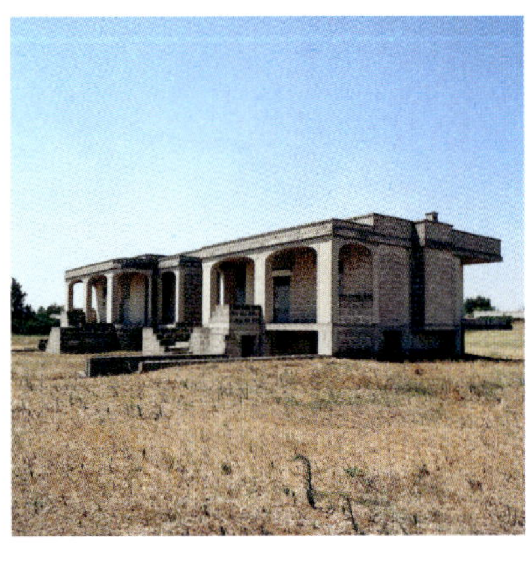

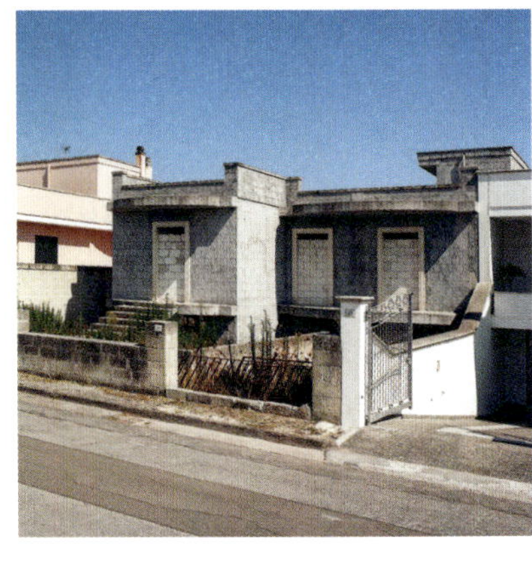
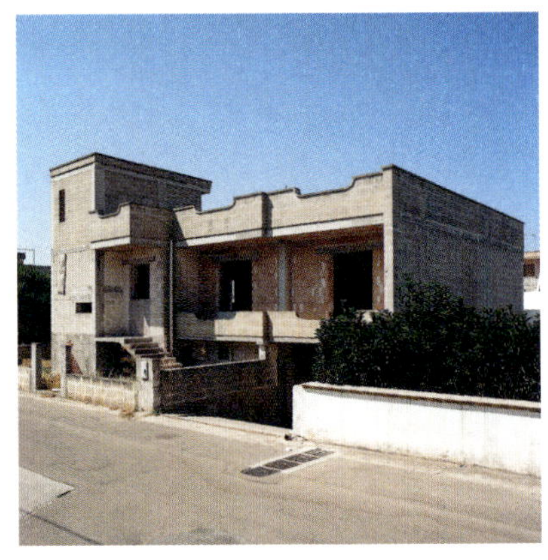
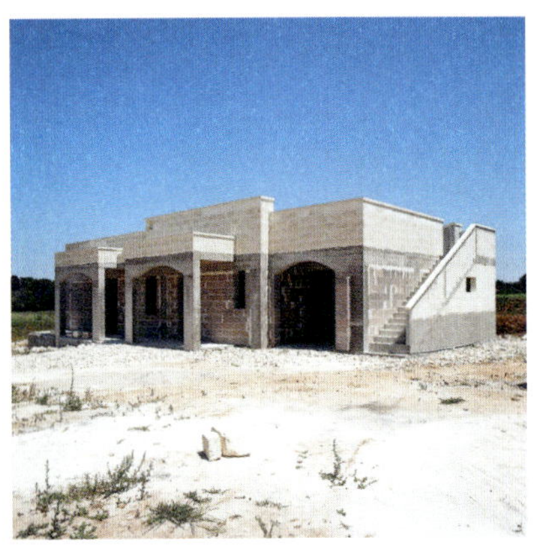
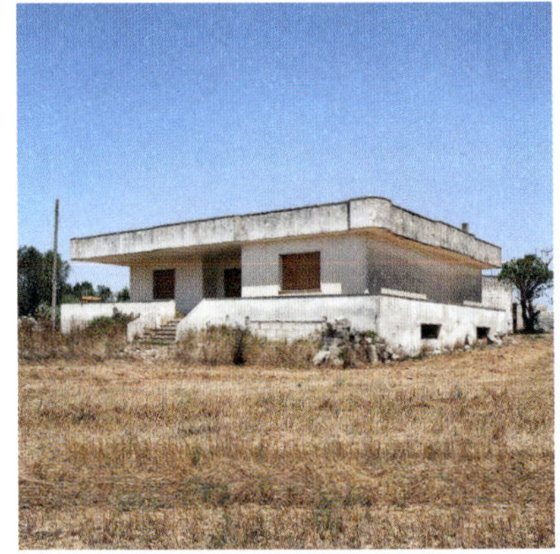
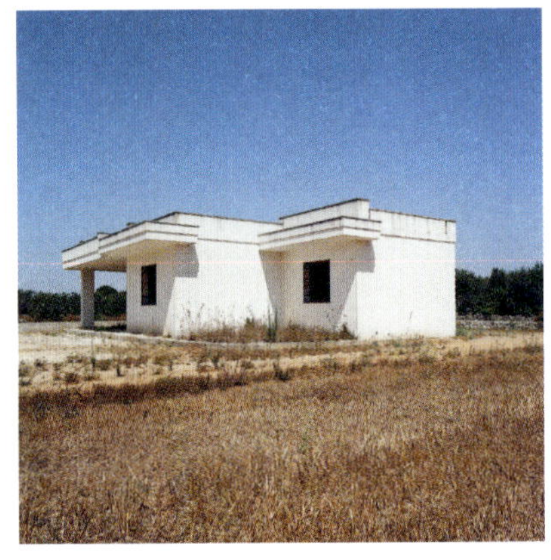
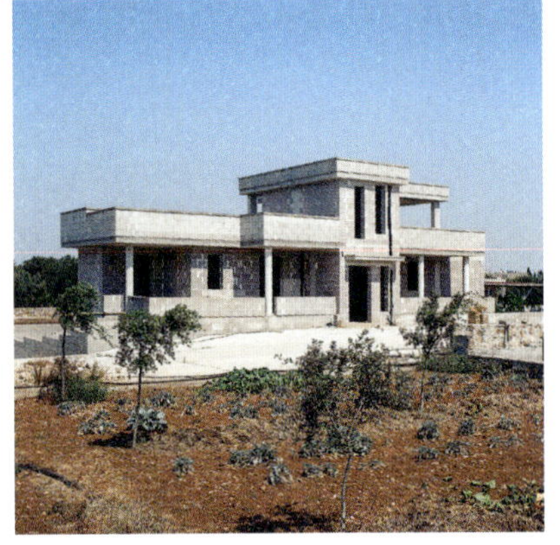
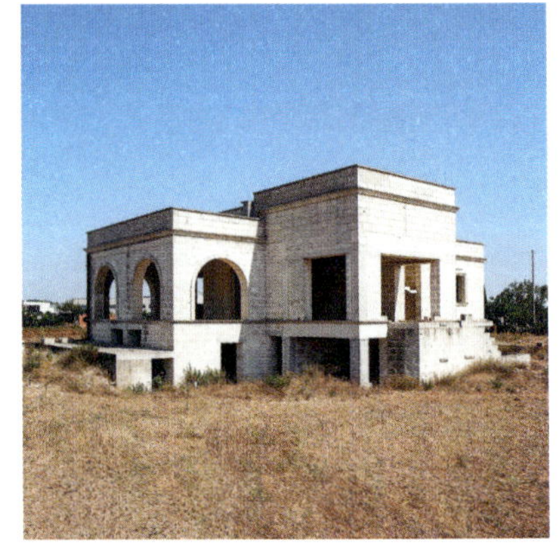
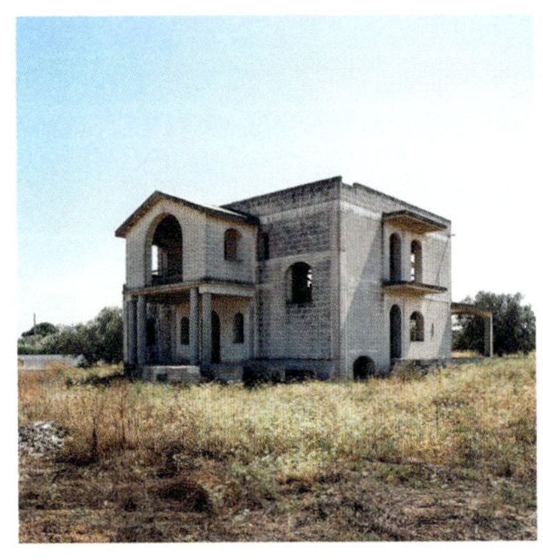
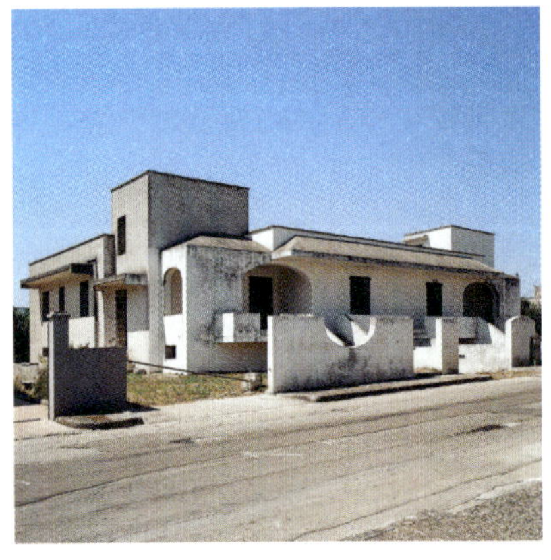
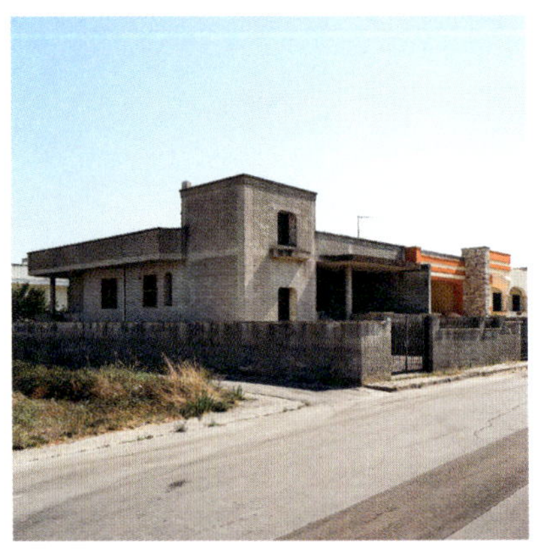
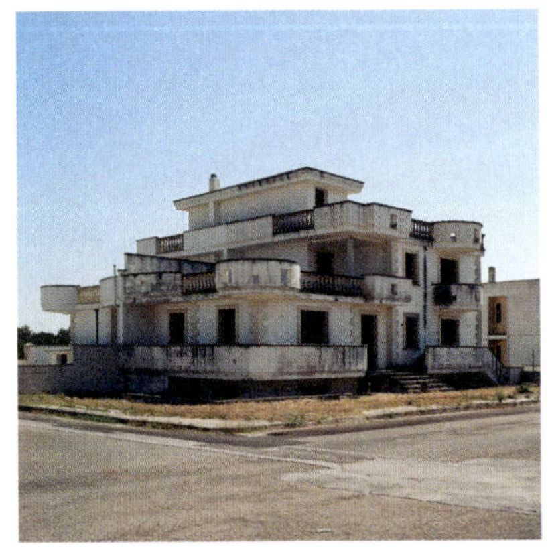
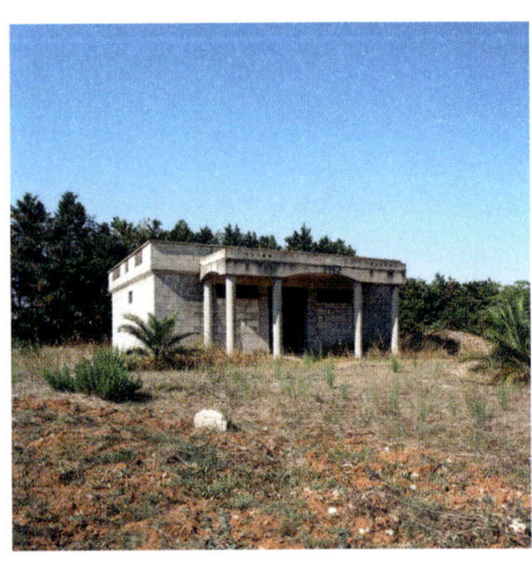

POGGIARDO

GIURDIGNANO

MOROMONTE

MINERVINO DI LECCE

SPECCHIA GALLONE

SOLETO

POGGIARDO

CANNOLE

CERFIGNANO

POGGIARDO

SANARICA

PALMARIGGI

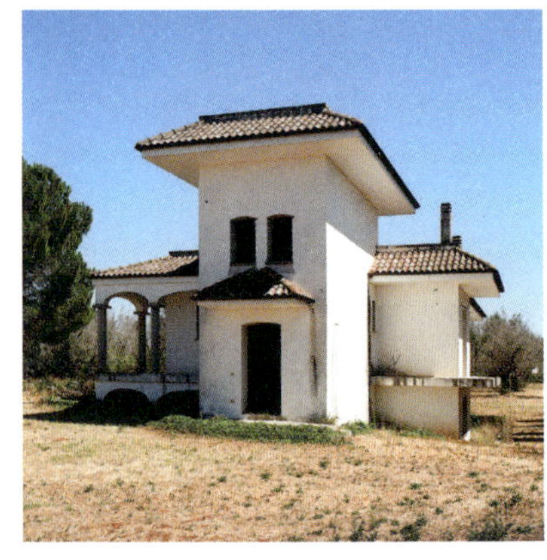 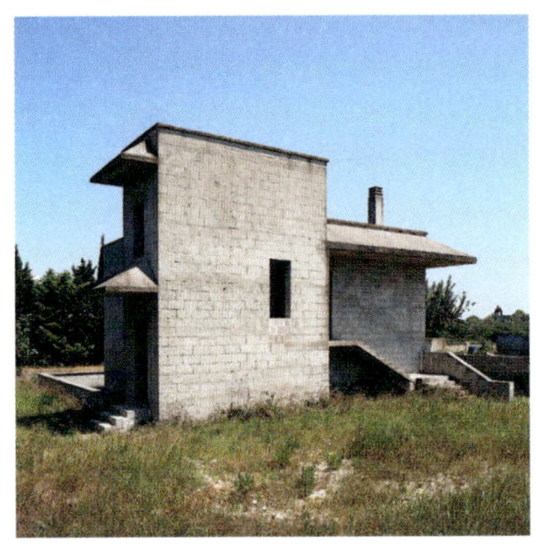 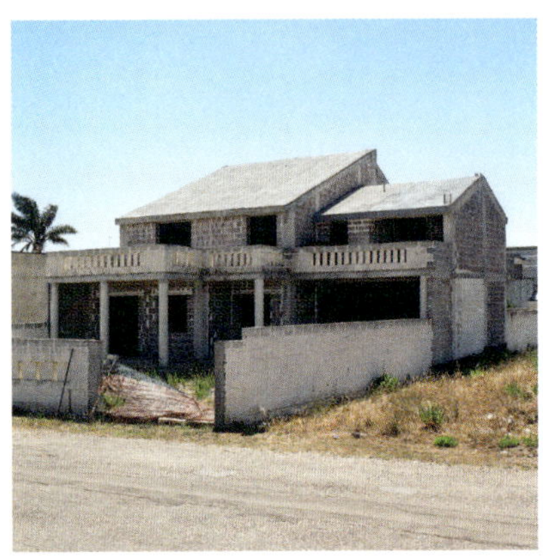
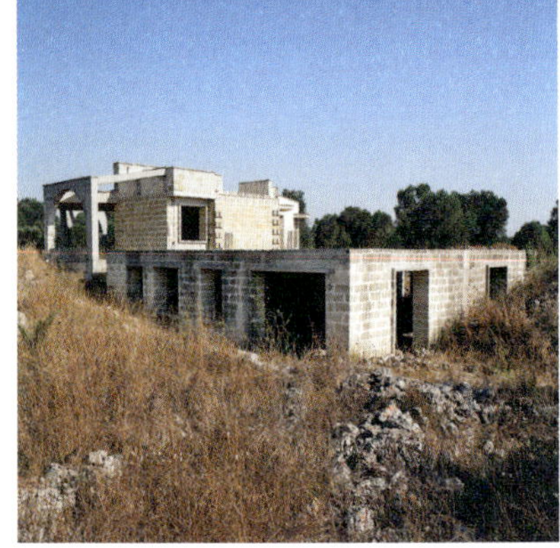 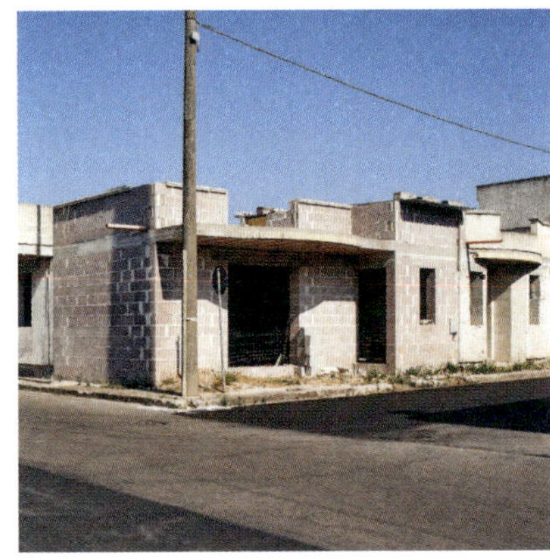 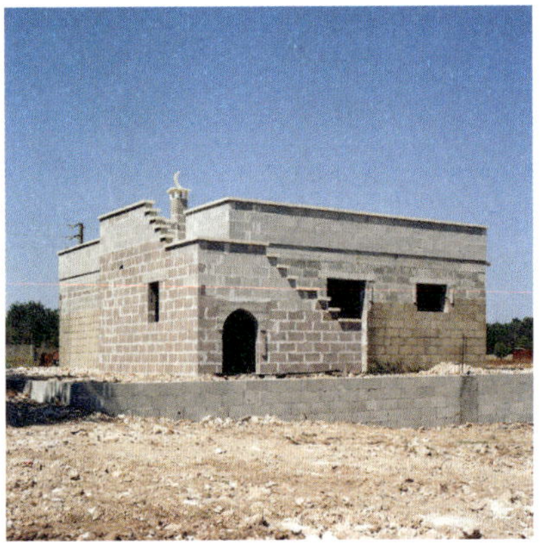
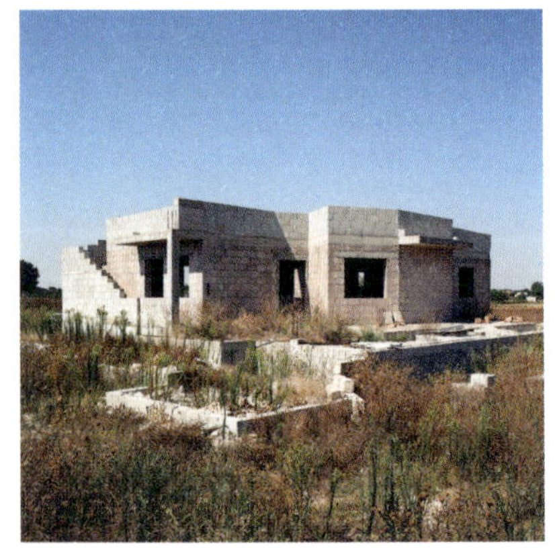 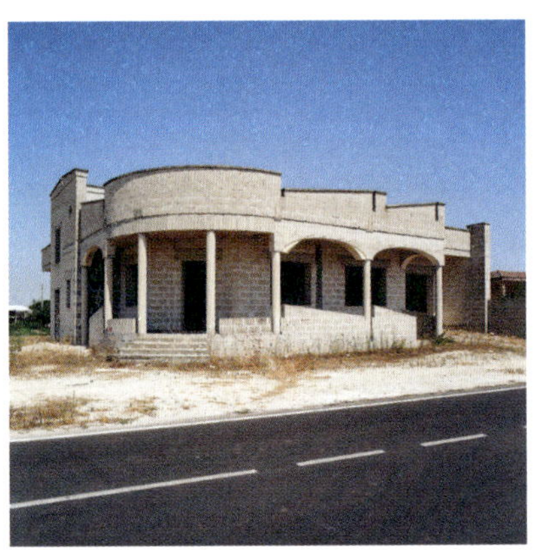 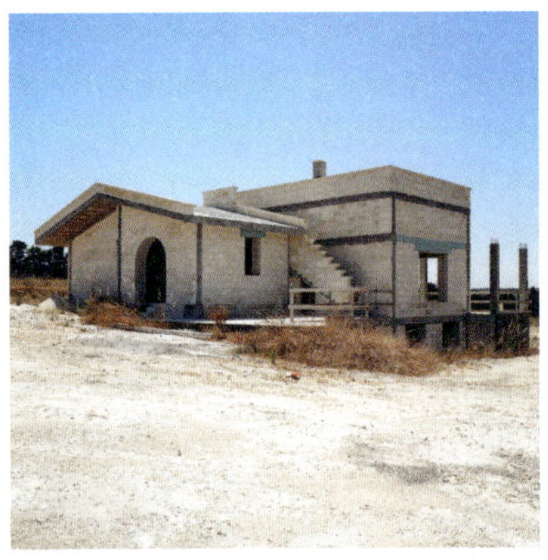
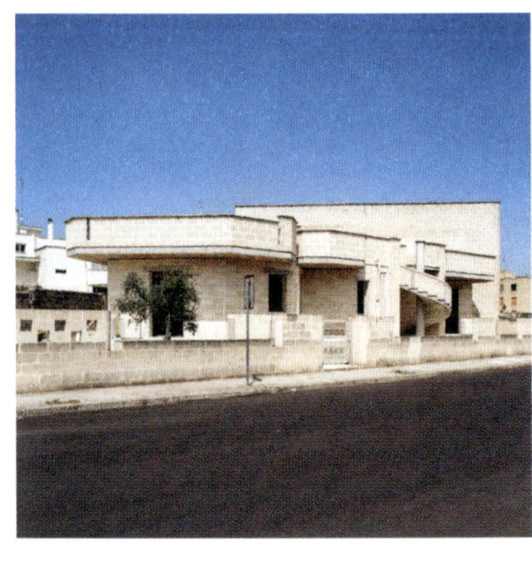 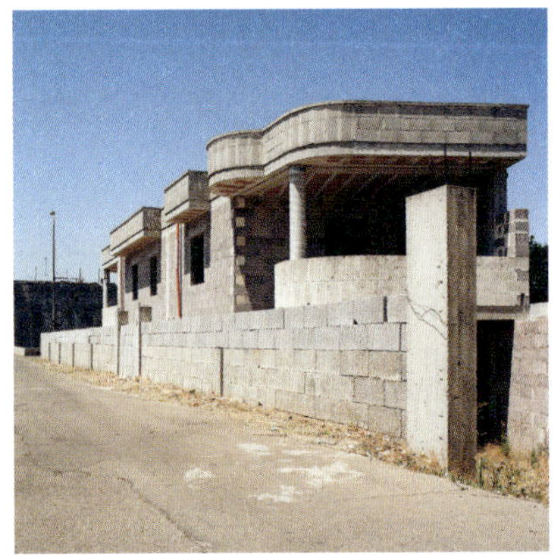 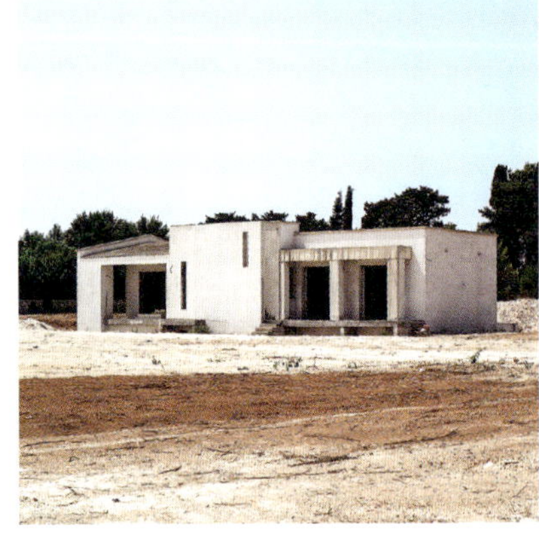

SAN CASSIANO

UGGIANO LA CHIESA

SCORRANO

MURO LECCESE

UGGIANO LA CHIESA

VITIGLIANO

GIUGGIANELLO

CASAMASELLA

ALIMINI

MARTANO

MINERVINO DI LECCE

ALIMINI

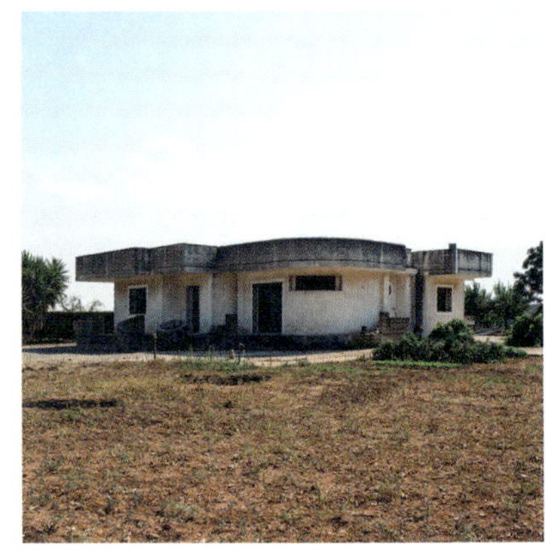
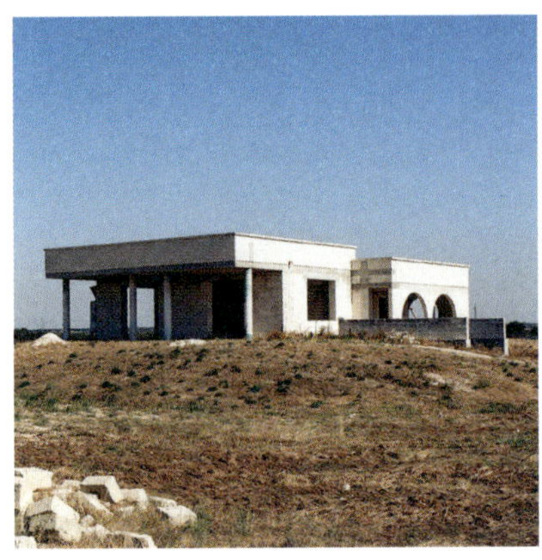
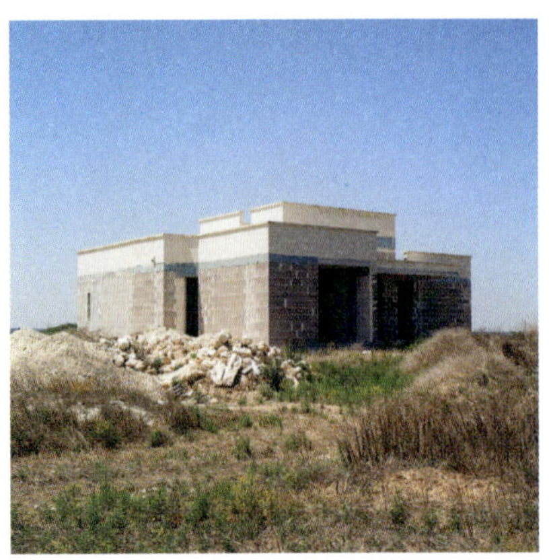
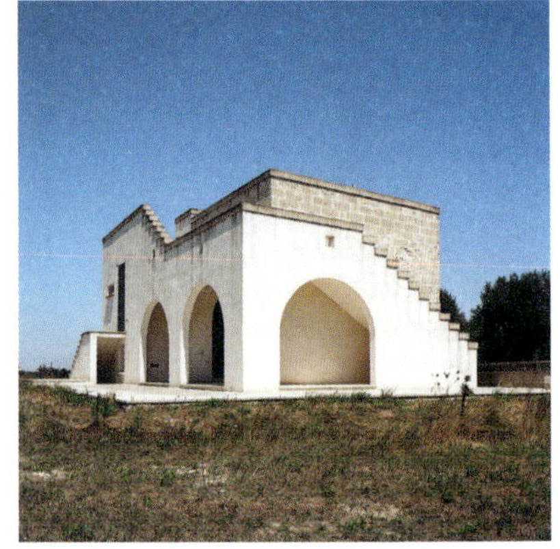
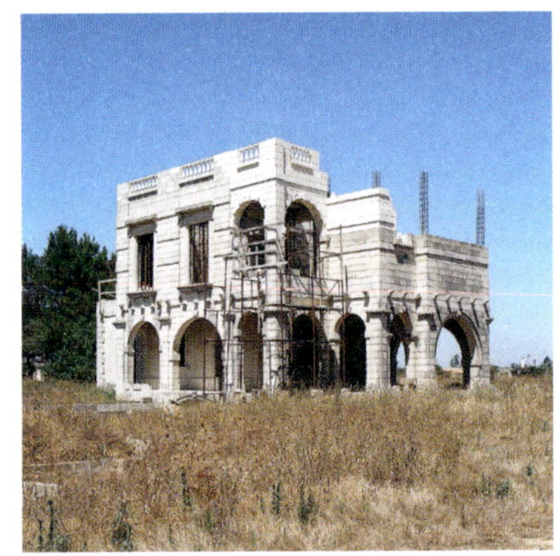
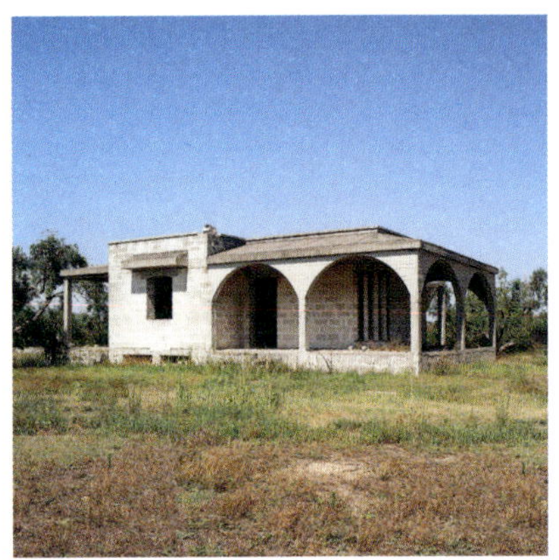
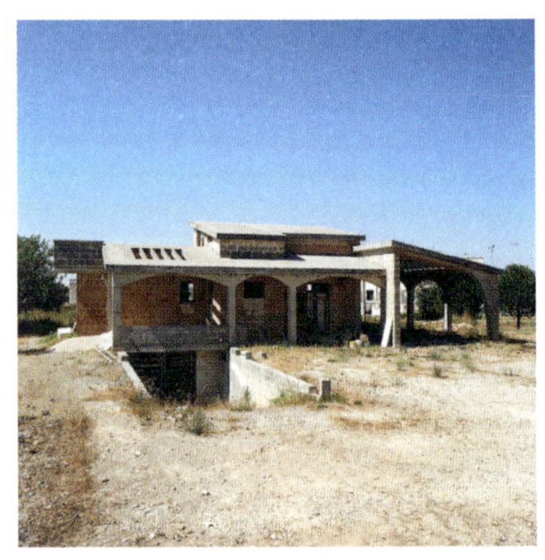
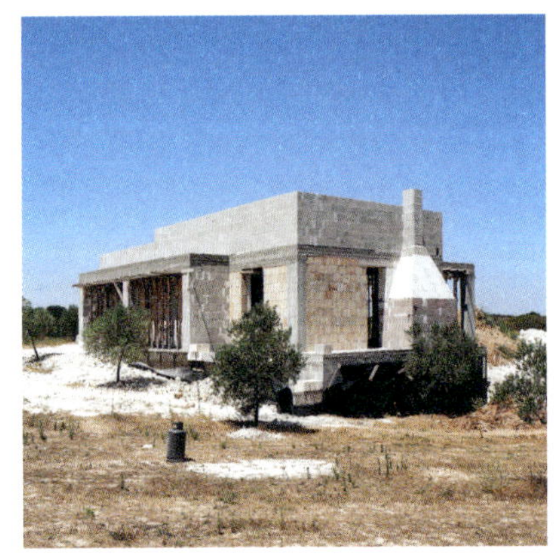
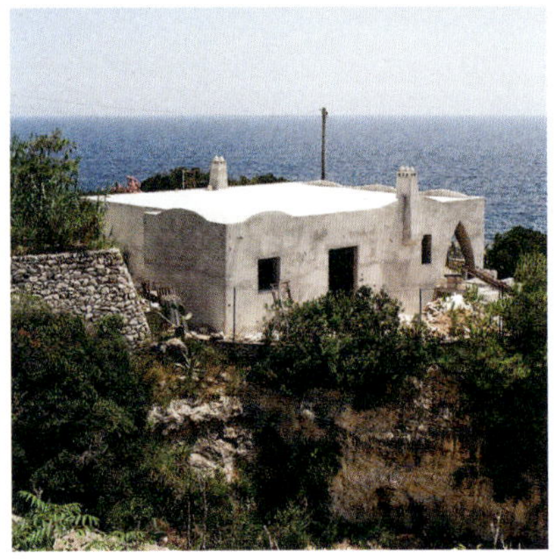
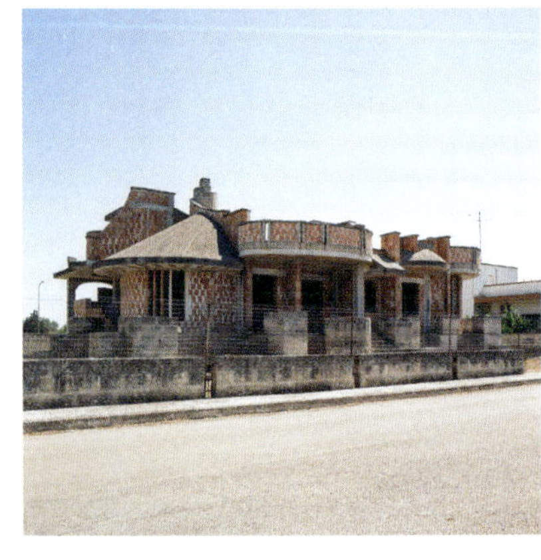
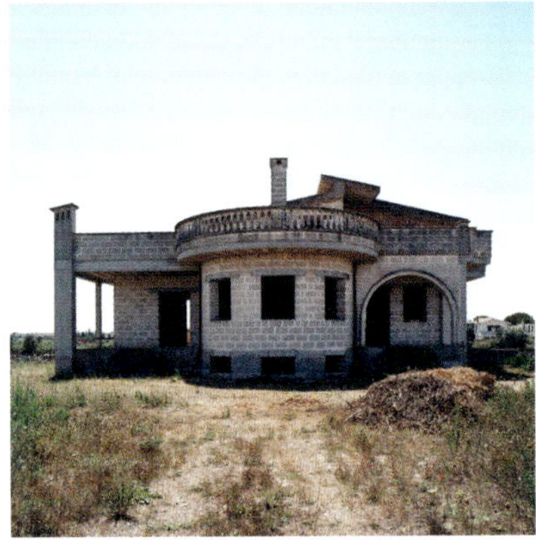

MURO LECCESE	PALMARIGGI	OTRANTO
PORTO BADISCO	SCORRANO	ZOLLINO
SPONGANO	MOROMONTE	TRICASE PORTO
ZOLLINO	STERNATIA	

HOMES ON HOLD

FOR ELÉA AND LIV

TRAVEL DIARY

Travel Diary contains a selection of inspiring locations
and architecture that reflect the essence of Salento.
All of them were captured while scouting out subjects
for the "Homes on Hold" project.

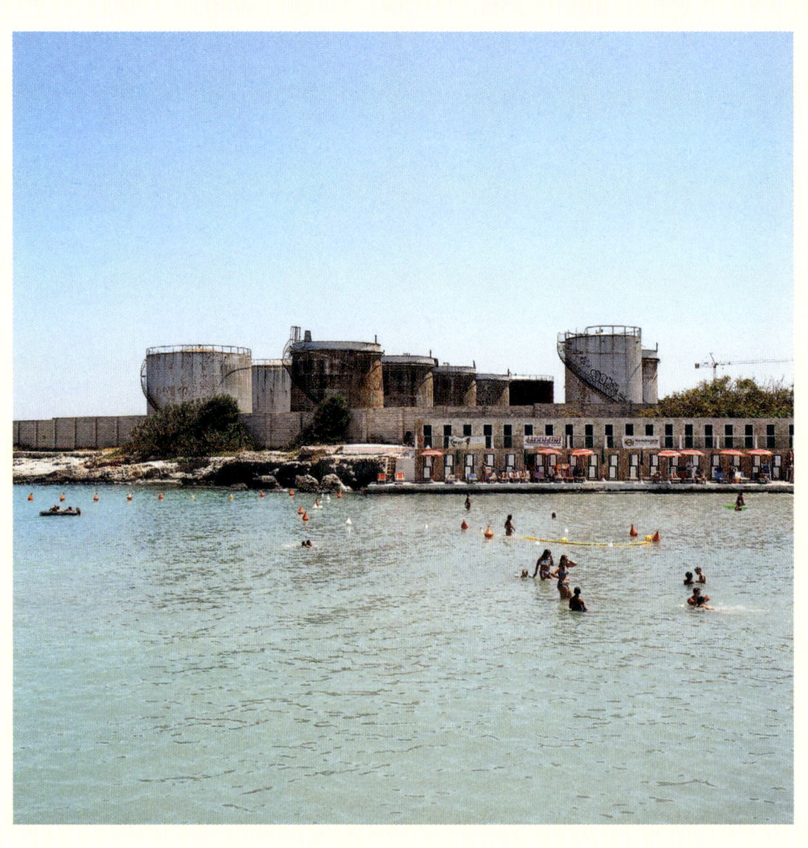

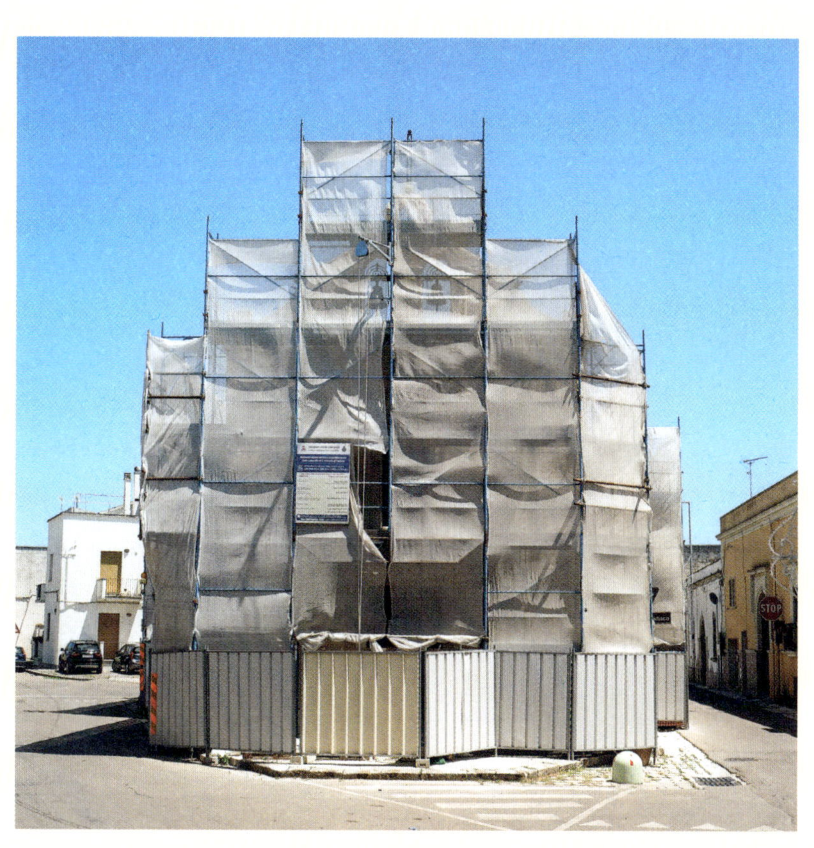

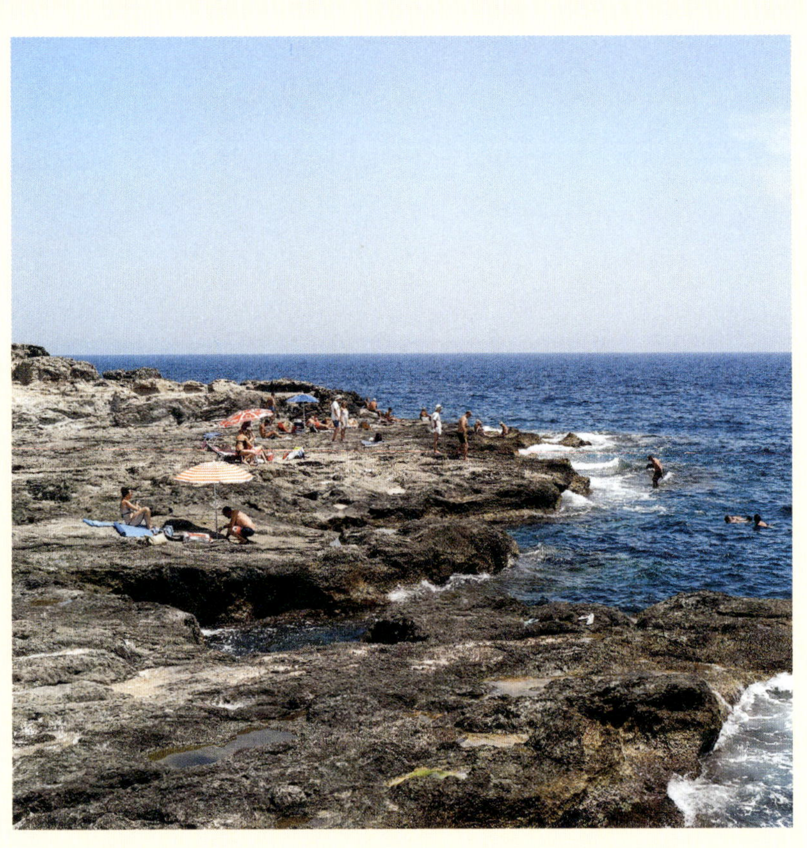

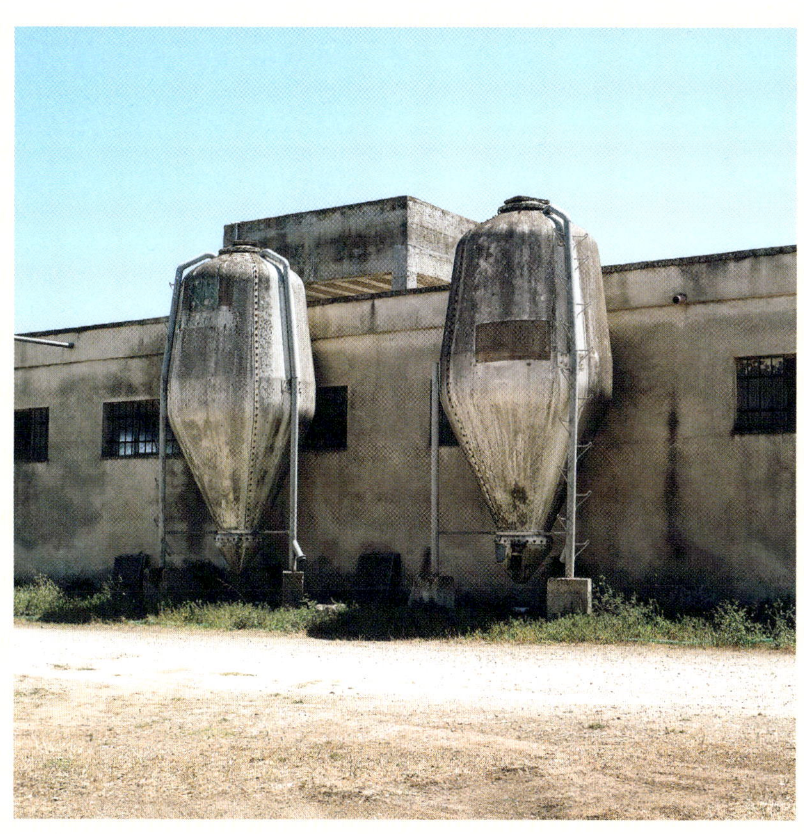

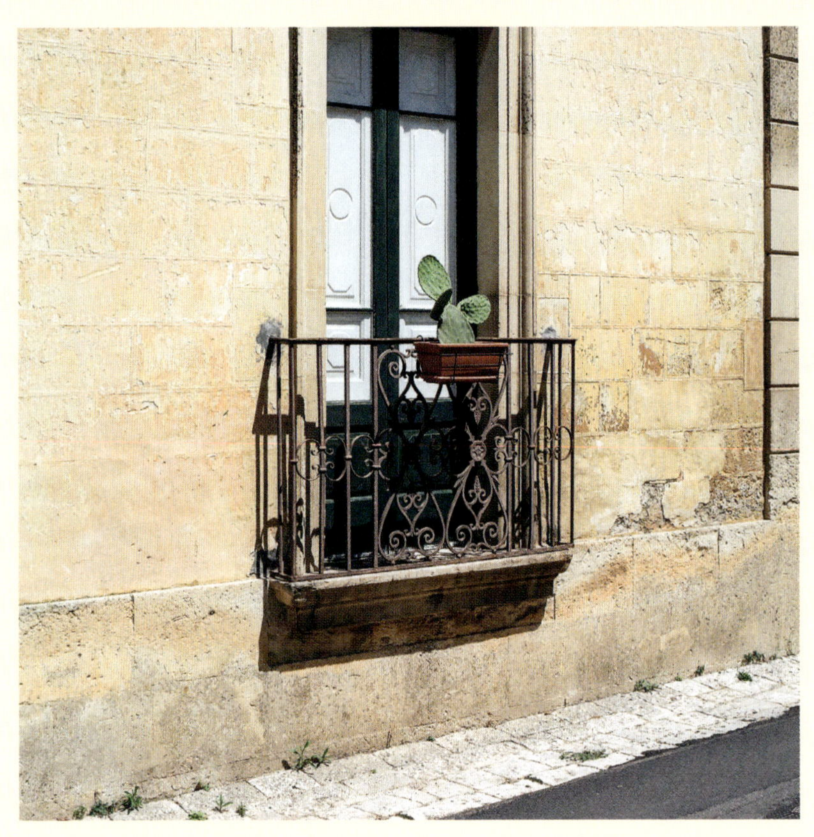

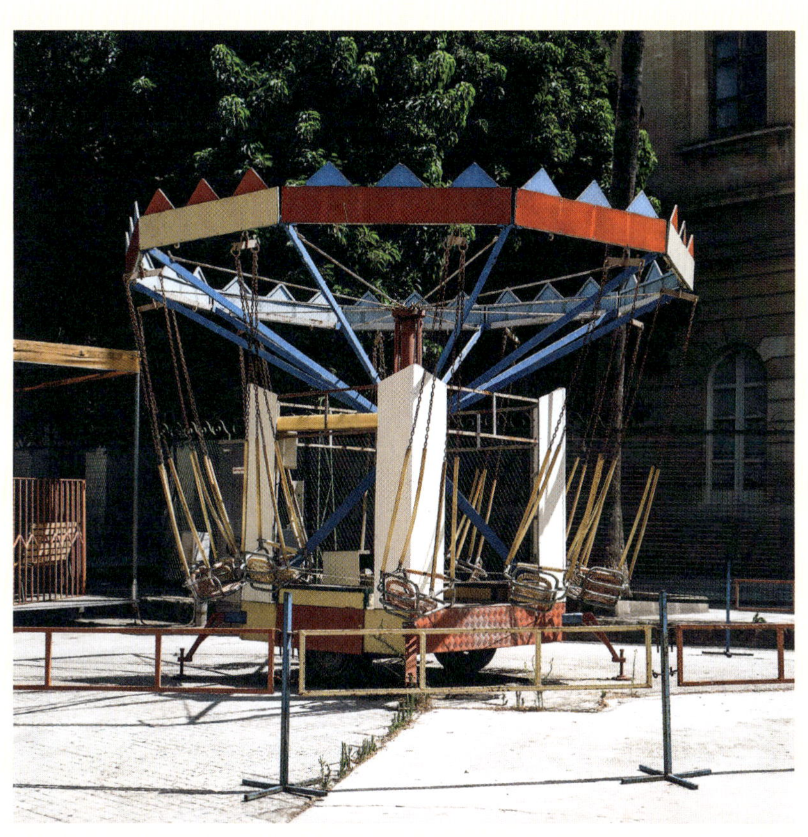

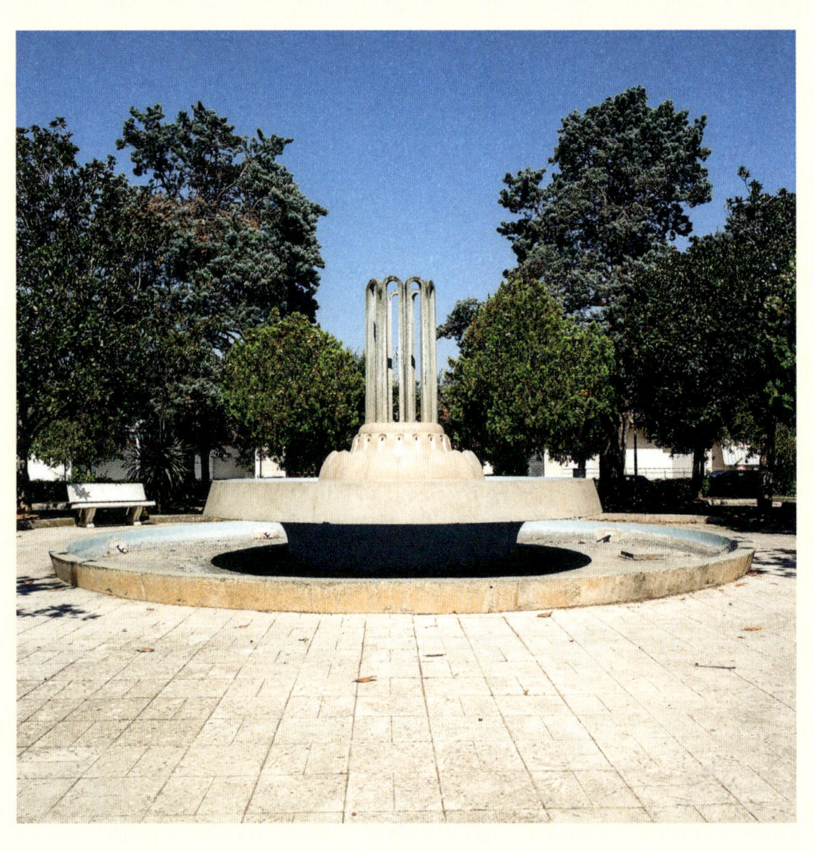

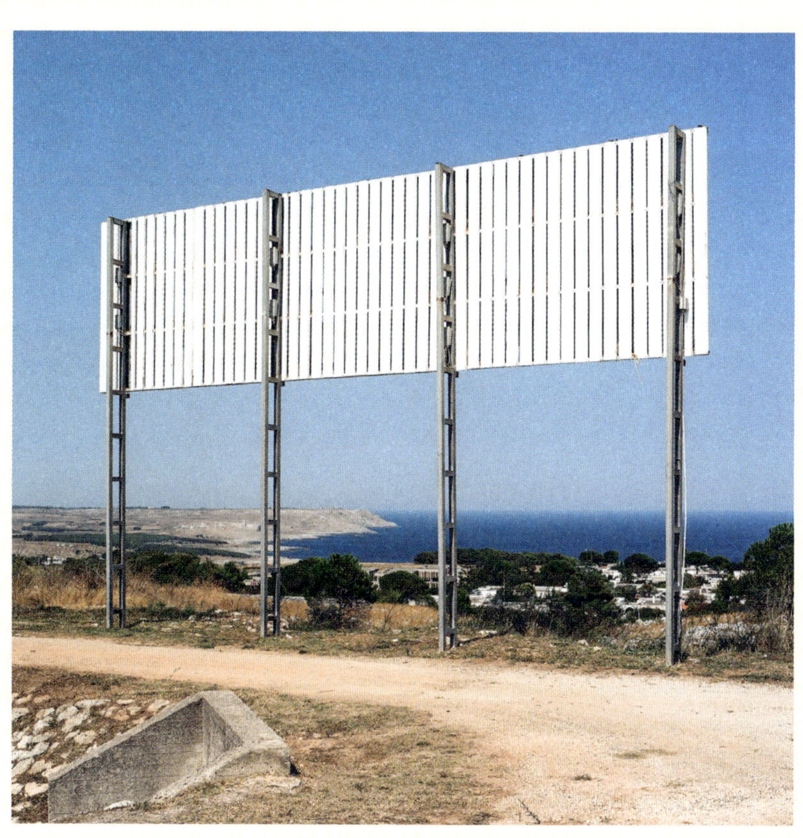

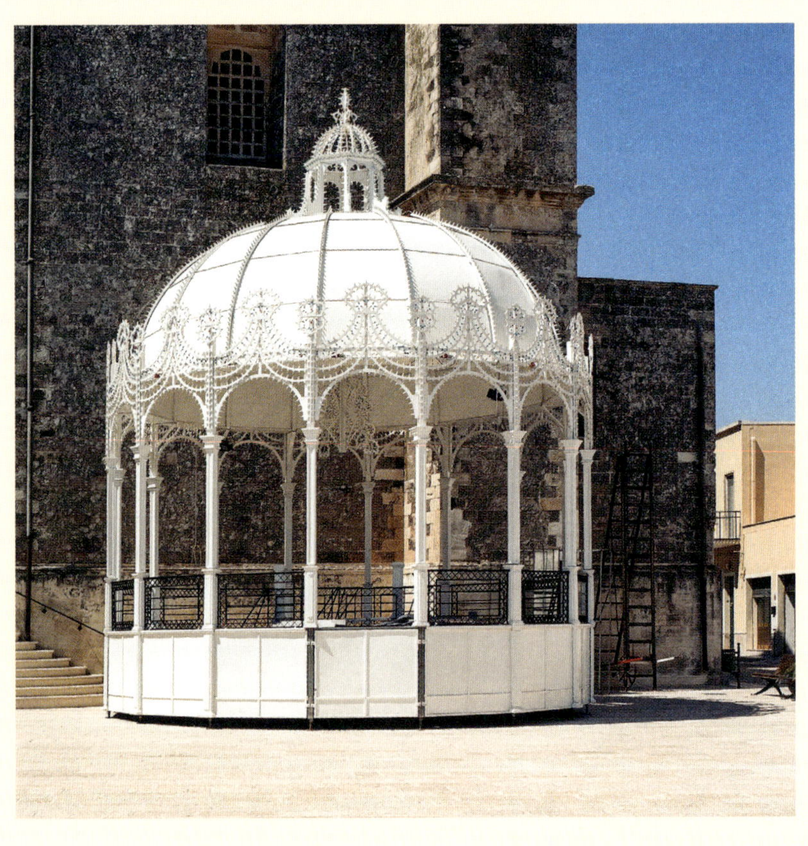

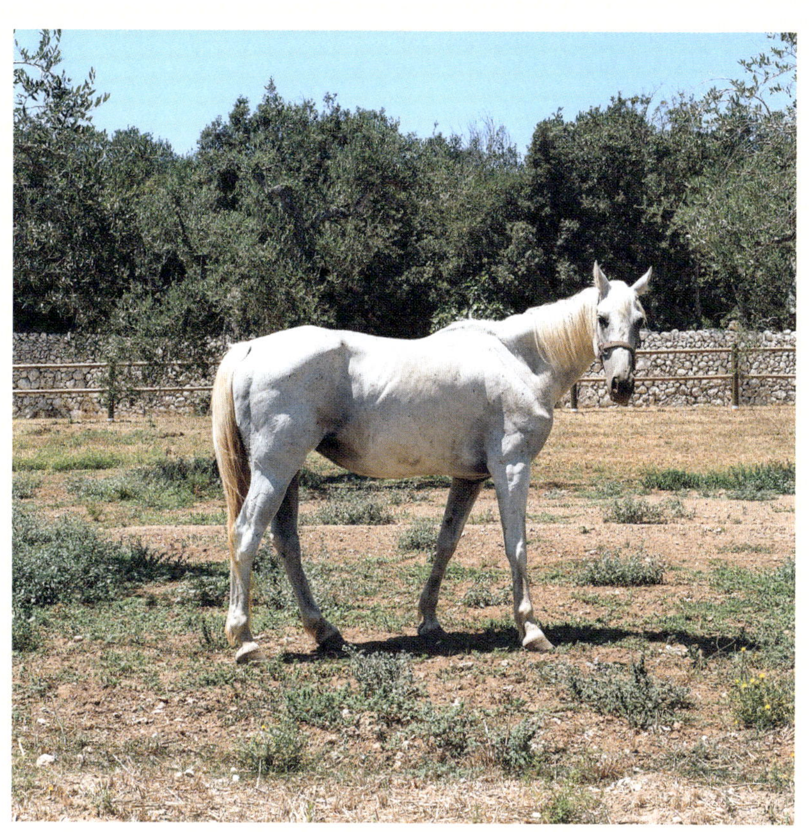

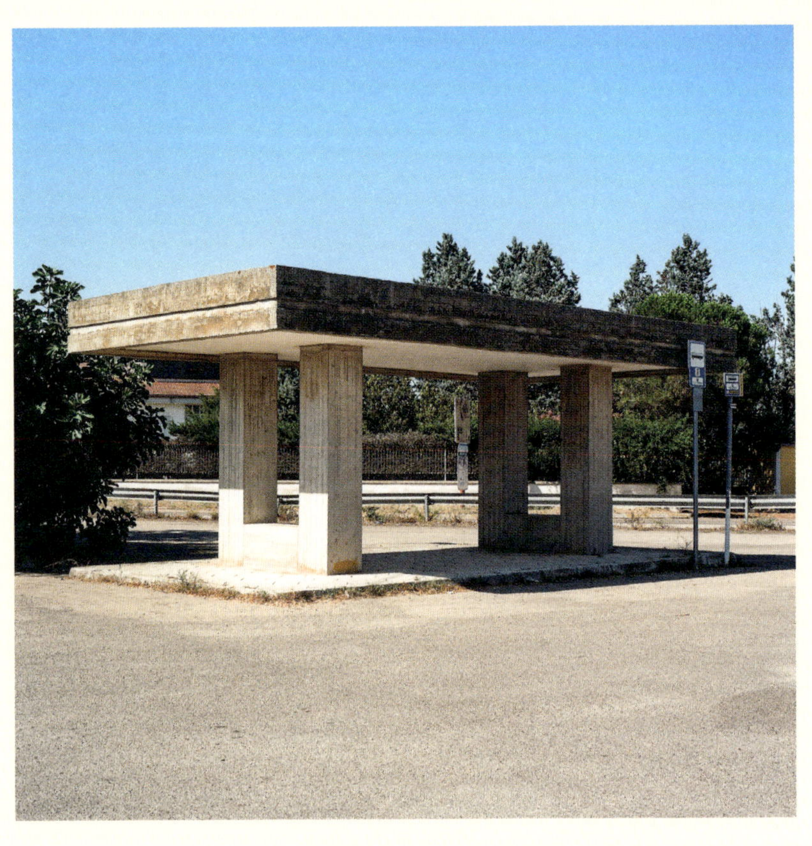

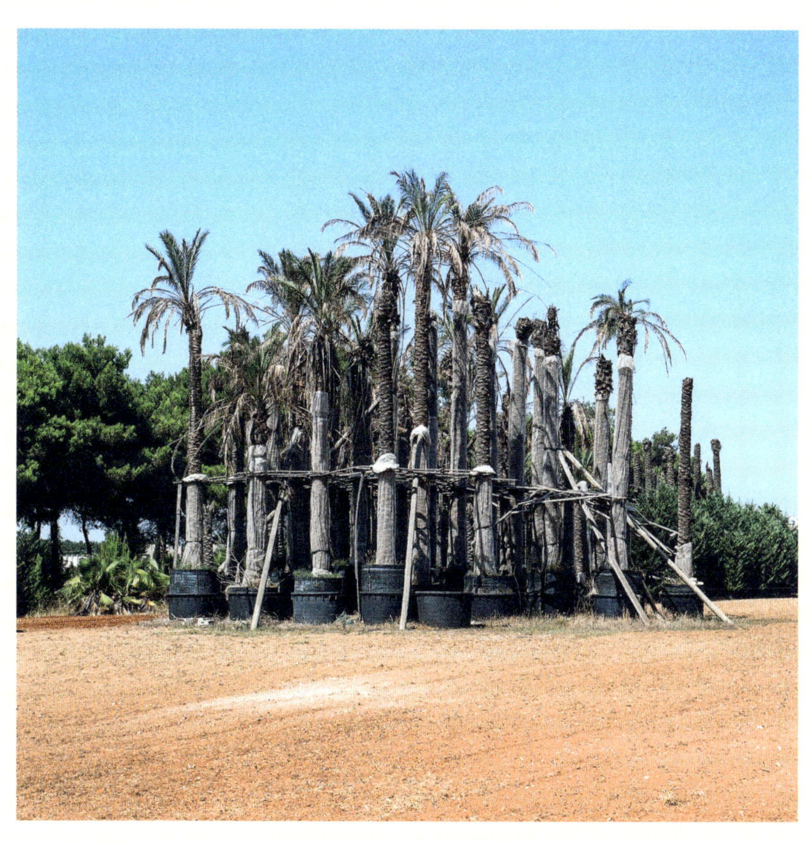

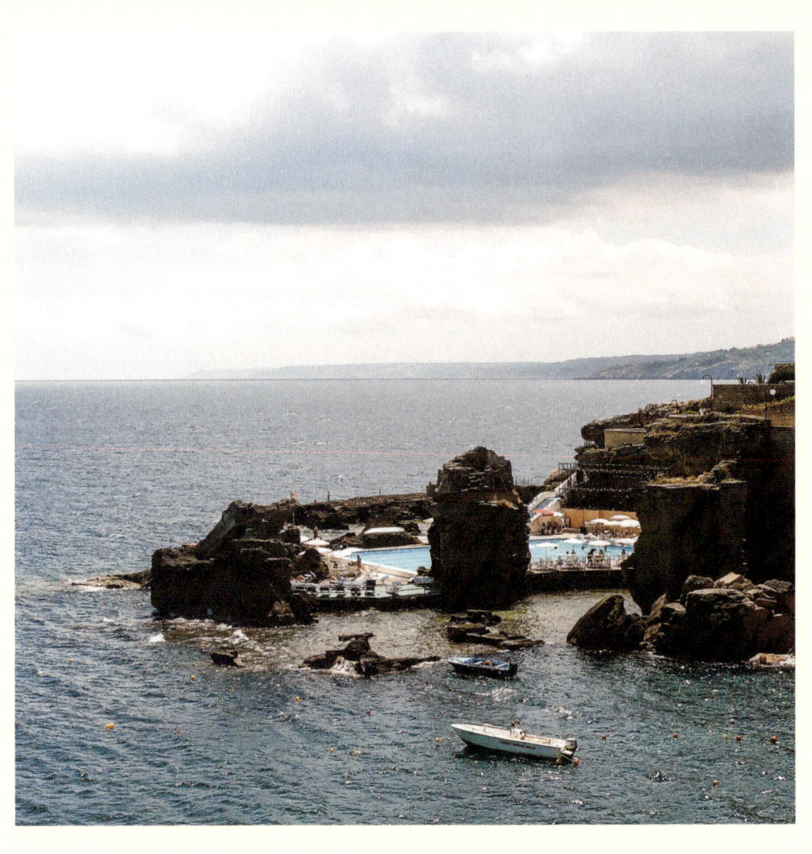

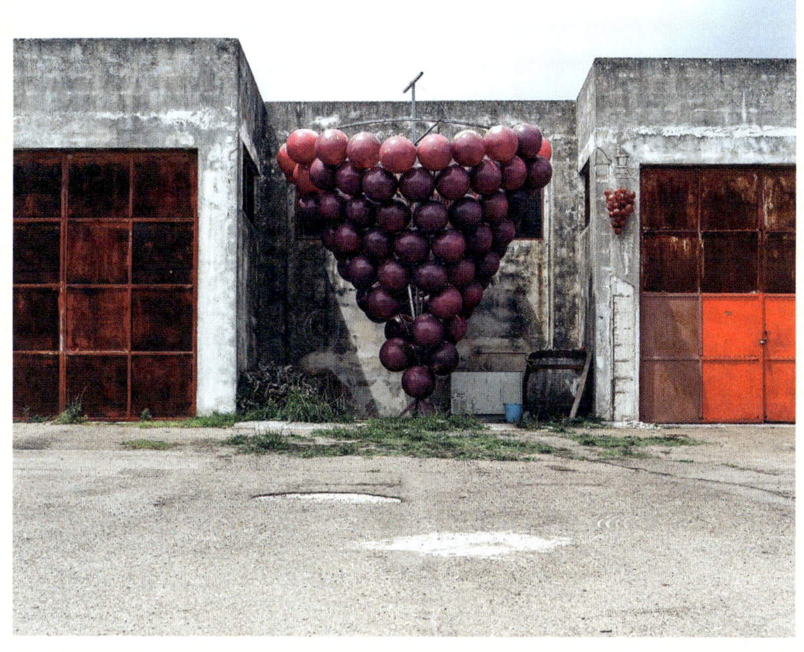

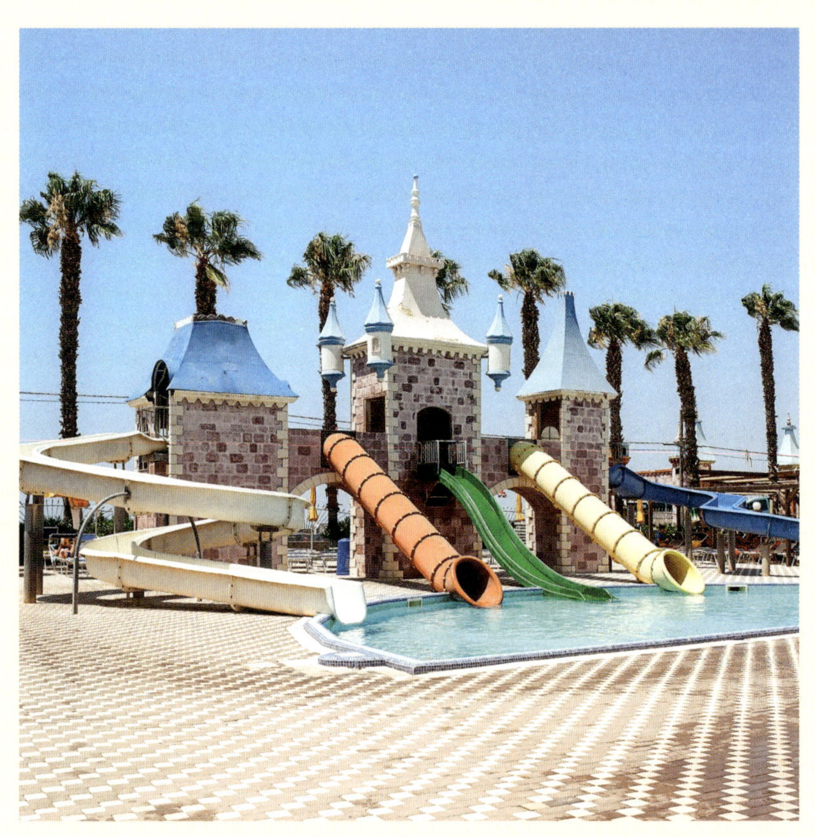

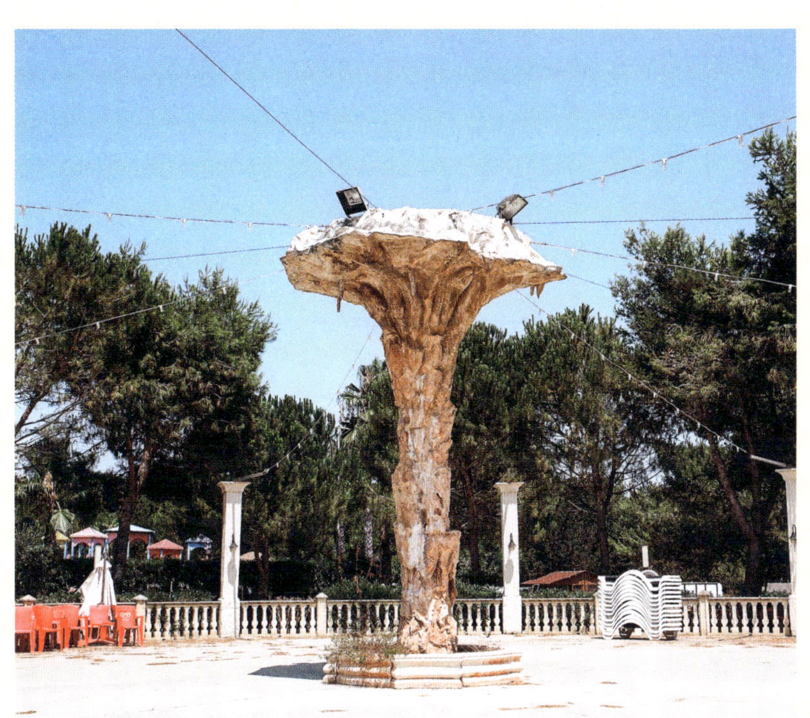

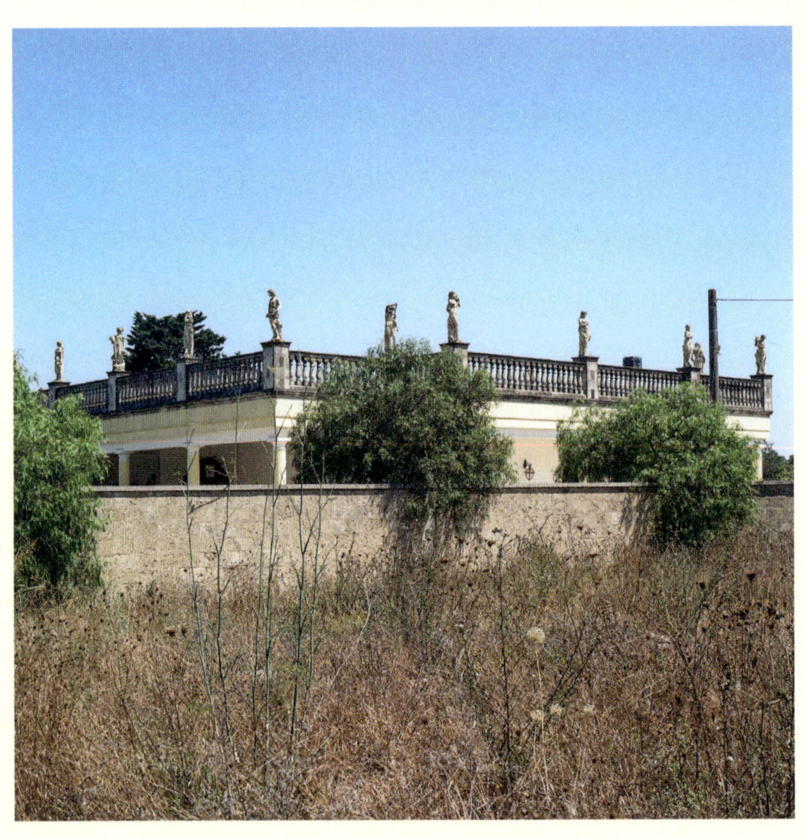

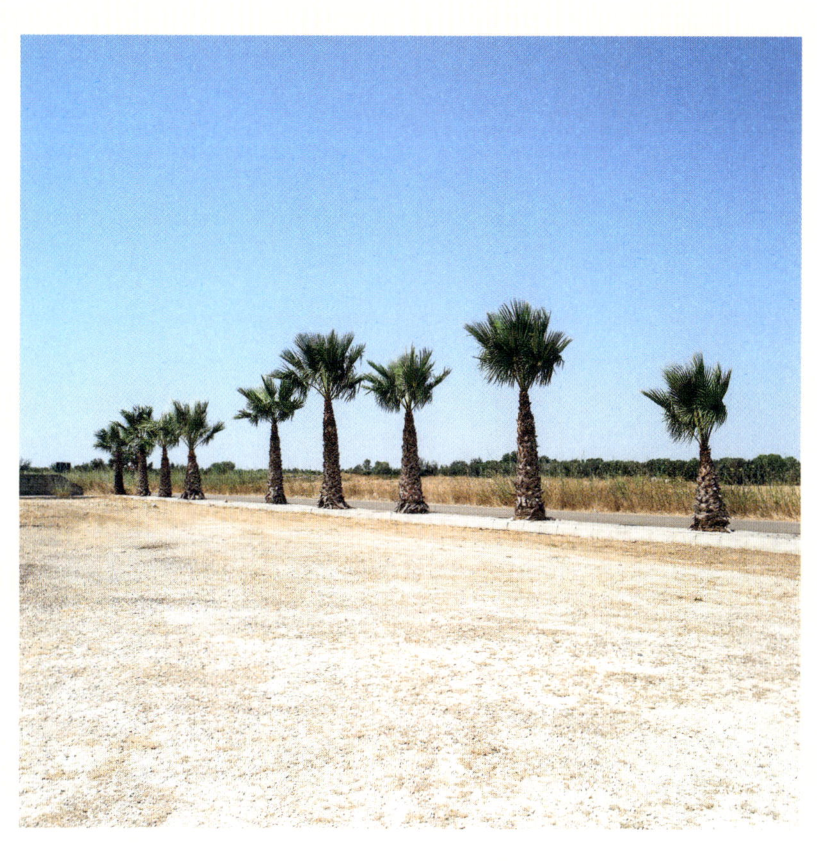

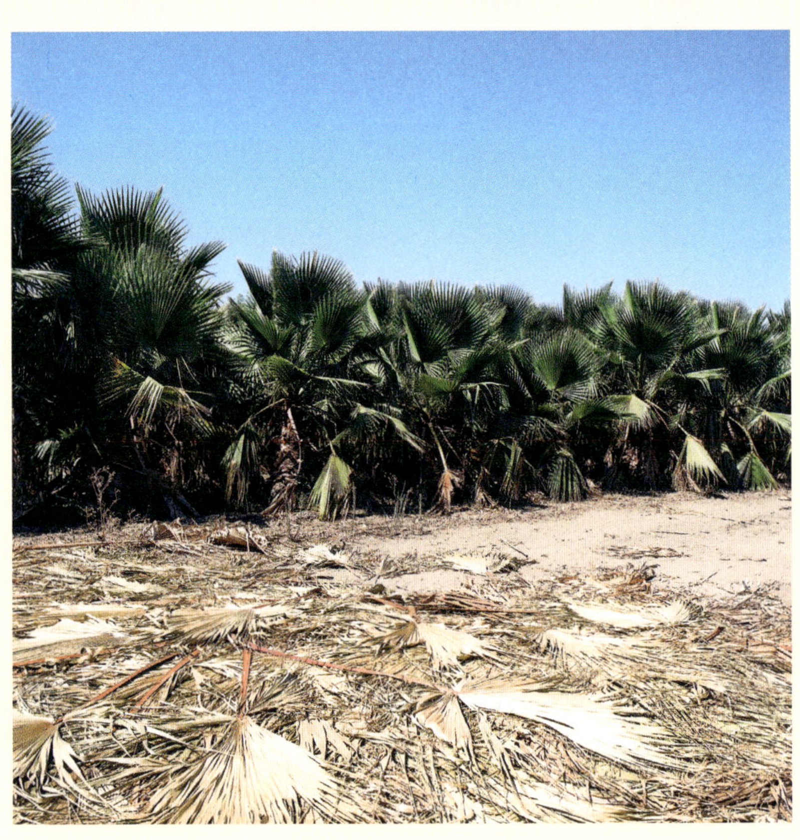

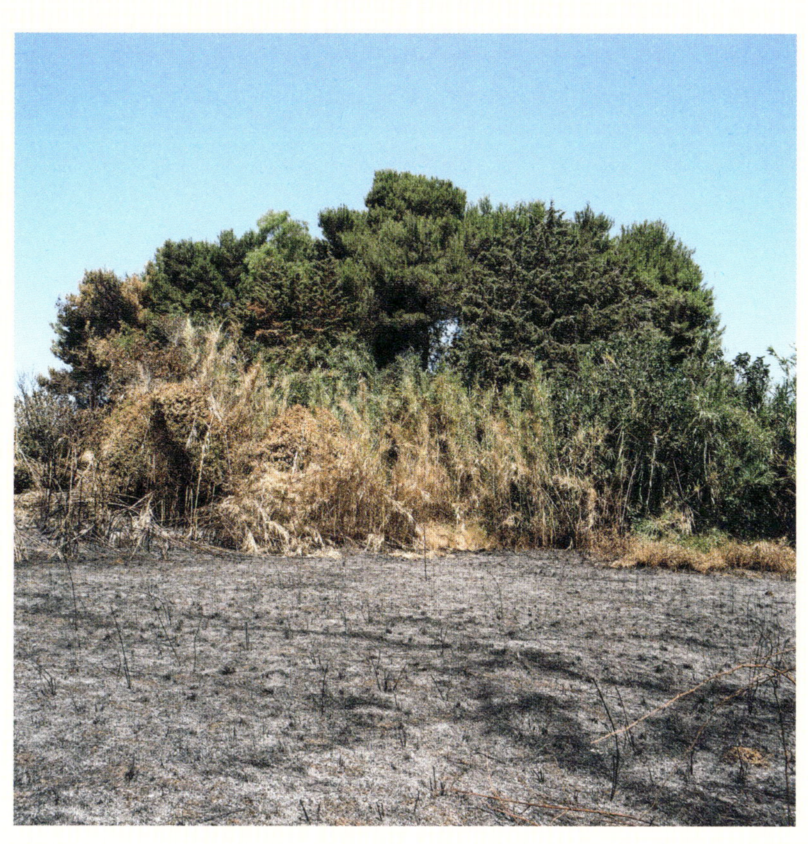

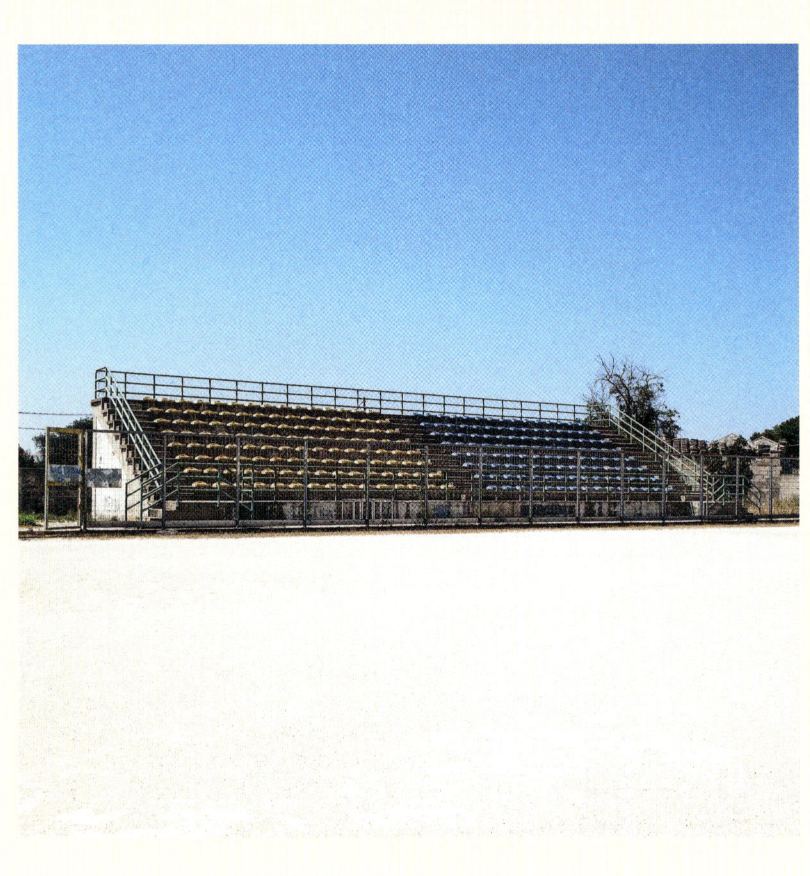

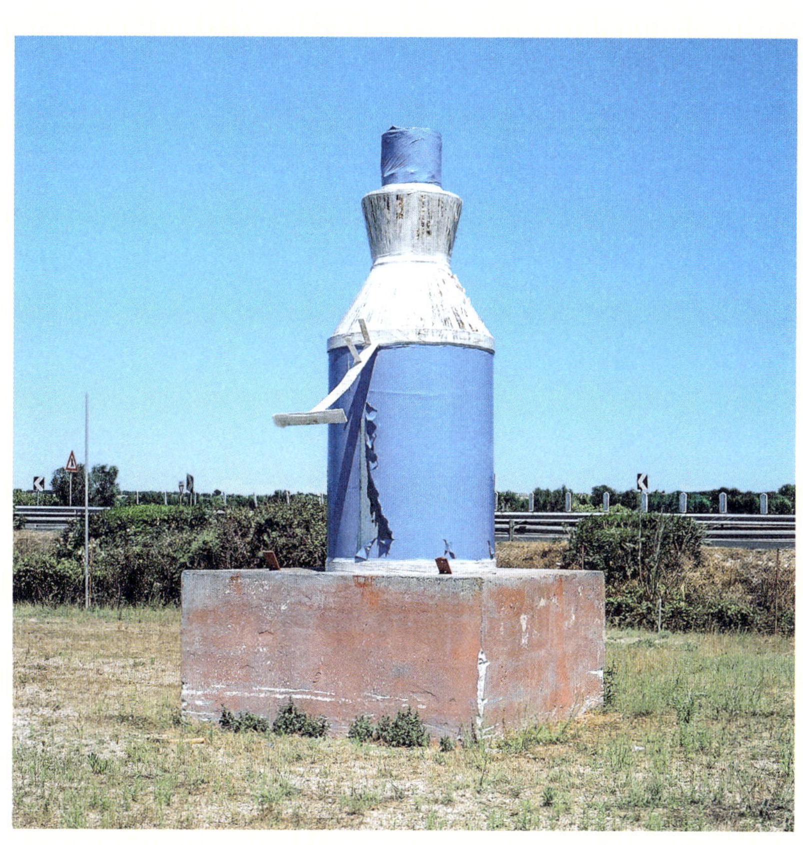

This book has been published with the wonderful support of
the Jan Michalski Foundation and Chambre Noire association.

**Fondation
Jan Michalski**

The Deutsche Nationalbibliothek lists this publication in the
Deutsche Nationalbibliografie; detailed bibliographic data are
available on the Internet at dnb.dnb.de

COLOPHON

HOMES ON HOLD –
TRACES OF UNFULFILLED DREAMS
Gabriel Mauron
Photographs from 2013 to 2021
gabrielmauron.com

EDITOR
BENTELI Verlag
benteli.ch

BOOK DESIGN
Dennis Moya
Gabriel Mauron

TEXTS
Anne Mauron
Francesca Giofrè - *Ph.D., Associate Professor, Sapienza University of Rome, Faculty of Architecture, Department Architettura and Design*
Fabio Quici - *Ph.D., Associate Professor, Sapienza University of Rome, Faculty of Architecture, Department of History, Representation and Restoration of Architecture*
Anna Bruna Menghini - *Ph.D., Associate Professor in Architectural and Urban Design, Sapienza University of Rome*
Mariangela Turchiarulo - *Ph.D., Associate Professor in Architectural and Urban Design, Polytechnic University of Bari*

TRANSLATION
Danielle Thien
Sandra Isabella

PHOTO EDITING
Scan Graphic SA

1st Edition 2023

ISBN 978-3-7165-1869-4

©2023 Benteli,
imprint of Braun Publishing AG, Salenstein